REVOLUTION UNDERWAY

REVOLUTION UNDERWAY

An Aging Church in an Aging Society

CEDRIC W. TILBERG

FORTRESS PRESS   PHILADELPHIA

69102

Library of Congress Cataloging in Publication Data

Tilberg, Cedric W.
  Revolution underway.

  Includes index.
  1. Church work with the aged. 2. Aged — United States.
I. Title.
BV4435.T55 1984   261.8'3426   84-8122
ISBN 0–8006–1817–3

K904D84   Printed in the United States of America   1–1817

To my mother and father,
who taught me how to grow old

Contents

Foreword

This volume is written with the conviction that the Lutheran Church in America and other parts of the religious community must take a new look at aging and the older adult. Vast demographic and social changes have been, are, and will be taking place in this dimension of life and society. Basic enough to be called a revolution, these changes are sure to have profound effects upon every facet of mission and ministry.

Part One, "Elders Today and Tomorrow," describes the most relevant of these changes. Part Two, "The Church's Response," addresses theological imperatives and then turns to the implications of the revolution for congregational life, the church's health and welfare agencies and institutions and educational programs, and regional judicatories and churchwide agencies.

Appreciation is expressed to staff members of the Department for Church in Society, Division for Mission in North America, for reviewing successive drafts of this study and sharing their insights and criticism; to Dr. Paul L. Brndjar, director for Church in Society and Dr. Kenneth C. Senft, executive director of the DMNA; to the DMNA management committee, which approved the document for publication and made valuable suggestions; and to a considerable number of readers in and beyond the LCA whose perceptive observations and encouragement have supported me in this effort. Thanks are also extended to Lillian Doe and Lorna Stevens for preparing the drafts of the manuscript.

Cedric W. Tilberg
Department for Church in Society
Division for Mission in North America
Lutheran Church in America

Introduction

This is a book about life, and it is a book about aging. Aging is an intrinsic part of living. All who live go through aging; they go through it all their years.

Older people are simply people who have traveled farther along the road of life. As they move into the later years, a new opportunity opens up before them, the opportunity to be harbingers of a new way of life. To the degree that elders grasp this opportunity, they will be in conflict with the way of life that pervades the contemporary world.

Society is dominated by a culture that exalts achievement, acquisition, and profit. It talks about doing things and getting things. It speaks of planned obsolescence (If cars are out-of-date in three or four years, why not people, too?), productivity (Whatever does not appear useful is thrown away), and the work ethic (The value of a man or woman is derived from work, particularly paid employment).

Now along come people who do not fit in with the ruling motif. With few exceptions they do not acquire an abundance of the world's goods; instead of making profits they receive less than they did at other times in their lives. They are in some ways out-of-date, and there are those who might like them to be thrown away. Most older people have no remunerative job through which they might claim identity or worth.

These people are the elders. Too often they have surrendered to the dominant way of life that has saturated their thinking, feeling, and acting since childhood. They have been a part of it, and it has been a part of them; they learned it as girls and boys, rebelled against it as adolescents, cooperated with it all their working years, and now, retired, they frequently allow that motif to be their tyrant, to crush them because they do not conform to its expectations. When this happens it is a human tragedy.

1

Let a challenge go forth to all older men and women to demonstrate an exciting new way of life, a way marked by the freedom to be themselves, to relate to other persons for their own sakes, to take time for things they truly want to do, to deal with suffering and loss in terms not of denial but of honesty and faith, and to walk humbly with their God.

If older adults respond affirmatively to this challenge, they will become the teachers of the generations that follow. By giving clues to a way of life that is yearning to be born, they will be defying the cultural assumptions on which modern society is built. Yet should not these assumptions be defied? Should not the freedom that becomes possible in the older years be present also at other stages of life?

Elders must be teachers. They must teach us all to face death as real and final, the end of all *unless* God's victory destroys death. Elders must lead us to see not only dying and death but crucifixion and resurrection. They must help us to view life as defined by mortality, by the limit of death.

No matter what our age, we all confront the imminent possibility of death — today, tomorrow, next year, half a century from now. But those older women and men who are aware of reality know the relentlessly increasing probability of death. They are called not to plunge into despair but to confess and witness to a triumphant faith. The more keenly they realize that, for them, less time is ahead than has gone before, the greater is the intensity of each moment. As death is beyond their control, and as the moments of life are also beyond their control, elders must be ready to place themselves in the hand of God and to accept life as the gift of God.

How much older persons should be able to teach us about life! But will they? The challenge is given to them to help people of younger ages discover a new way of life, a way that gives them freedom to understand the heights and the depths of human experience, a way that enables them to look with a clear eye at the culture ruling our world and expose what is superficial and evil in it.

The challenge also goes forth to all other people. We must *listen* to elders and *hear* what they have to say. So often we deal with them in a manner that makes their teaching impossible. We are so busy ministering to them that we cannot receive their ministry to us. This is true in society. It is true also in the church.

The Purpose of This Book

This book is an expression of concern about both personal and societal aging. A nation or a society is aging when the average age of its people rises. This has been happening in the United States and Canada as the result of the demographic combination of falling birthrates and rising life expectancy in both nations. The number of men and women age 65 and over has been rising dramatically for many years. It will rise even more dramatically in the second decade of the twenty-first century when the vanguard of the "baby-boom" generation (persons born between 1946 and 1965) begin turning 65. There will then be many more older people in North America, and they will represent a higher proportion of the total population.

At the same time the social meanings of growing older are being altered: Retiree and elder are being recognized as new stages in the life cycle. The social environment and the characteristics of older adults are changing and will change even more.

These features of societal aging will be discussed in Part One, "Elders Today and Tomorrow." The presence of older people is everywhere evident; the question is whether either church or society is adequately prepared for their impact.

Societal aging has been called an "iceberg issue" in our history. "The tip has been known for decades, but its deeper outlines and implications are only beginning to be fathomed."[1] Most people think of aging as a personal fate rather than a public issue. Biologists and psychologists, for a long time the only interested scholars, have dealt with aging within the boundaries of their disciplines. Politicians and others seeking legislation favorable to elders have presented their case as nonpartisan and, therefore, noncontroversial. Churches and other religious organizations have approached the older population primarily as individuals who have problems that call for service, care, and comfort.

It is time to recognize that a revolution is underway. "It's a revolution that is still in its early stages but which will inexorably and inevitably succeed in changing the way we think and act. . . . It is the revolution of the old."[2]

Aging is a societal issue of the first magnitude.[3] Are we as individuals or as the corporate church aware of what is happening?

Are we prepared to face up to it? The church, facing aging and the older adult as a societal issue, should respond in new and creative fashion to (1) the force of the demographic transition now in progress; (2) the changes taking place in elders today and tomorrow; and (3) the imperatives of its theology. The first two are considered in Part One of this book; the third is discussed in the opening section of Part Two. Possible responses of the church are dealt with in Part Two.

These responses will be more intelligent if informed by a history of aging in recent centuries. To that subject we now turn.

Aging in America—A Brief History

David Hackett Fischer[4] identifies five stages in the history of attitudes toward aging in the United States. The overlapping of the stages emphasizes that we must guard against oversimplification when dealing with historical trends. Changes did not occur suddenly. The transition periods were times when deep social currents began to move in new directions, the results of which often became evident only in later years.

First Stage:
Exaltation of Age (1607–1820)

During this long period older adults, though relatively few in number, controlled the land and frequently exploited the young. Since older people ruled in society, public and church leaders stayed in office until death. The young were trained to venerate age, but this veneration was not necessarily warmed by affection. Elders, the keepers and transmitters of the culture, held the seats of highest honor in New England meetinghouses, both secular and religious. In hair styles and clothing, women and men tried to appear older than they were, and in census surveys some reported that their ages were beyond the fact.

Second Stage (Transition):
The Revolution in Age Relations (1770–1820)

Late in the eighteenth century the *direction* of change reversed. The social status of older persons began to fall. They lost the seats of honor in the meetinghouses. New laws called for retirement at a fixed age. Clothing and hair styles reflected youth rather than age, and some people told census takers that they were younger than they were. Increasing distribution of wealth gradually eroded the economic power of the old.

Third Stage:
The Cult of Youth in Modern America (1770–1970)

During the nineteenth century expressions of hostility toward old age became steadily stronger. The New England Transcendentalists —for example, Thoreau, Emerson, Margaret Fuller, and Bronson Alcott—were ardently committed to the cult of youth. Some Victorian literature continued to honor age, but in a different way from the Puritans. Now the old were "mementos of past virtue," weak and mellowed rather than stern and commanding. It appears that in many cases as veneration of elders declined, the bonds of personal affection—though not necessarily intimacy—became stronger between individuals of different generations.

Fourth Stage (Transition):
Old Age as a Social Problem (1909–1970)

Early in the twentieth century old age came to be seen as a problem — one among many — to be solved by the intervention of society through its chief tool, government. There was a slow development of pension programs, commissions on aging at various levels of government, and other efforts to attack the problems of the elderly. In 1935 the federal government, in the Social Security Act, acknowledged survival as a basic human right and the supply of the minimal means of subsistence to every individual as a social obligation. Other important legislation followed, for example, Medicare, Medicaid, and the Older Americans Act were all passed in 1965. A number of active organizations concerned with the problems of aging appeared, including the American Association of Retired Persons (AARP), the National Council on the Aging, and the National Caucus of the Black Aged. White House Conferences on Aging held in 1961, 1971, and 1981 also made impacts upon public policy. There was a proliferation of public and private homes for the aged, nursing homes, and other facilities which provide care for older persons. Geriatrics began to be identified as a medical specialty; and the social science of gerontology—although it at least goes back to approximately 1922 with G. Stanley Hall — started to flourish in the 1940s.

Fifth Stage:
A *Thought for the Future (1909–)*

In the late twentieth century we may be beginning a new and constructive period in relation to aging and the older adult. The church can make an important contribution to the realization of this new day. Knowing our history should protect us from simply working for a correction of the recent past, with its cult of youth and its depreciation of those who are older. It should protect us also from seeking a resurgence of the situation in early America, with its cult of age and its depreciation of the young. Is it possible to build a society and a church with a partnership of generations in which the profound differences between age and youth are respected and appreciated without creating a system of social inequality?

The new day in age relationships will require the enlargement of freedom of choice for elders (as well as for persons in the younger generations) in the job market, in location and type of living arrangements, and in personal associations. It will call for the destruction of inaccurate and demeaning stereotypes of both young and old, and the intentional cultivation of respect for the dignity of all human beings. In the fulfillment of these tasks the church has a significant opportunity and responsibility, both in its own life and in the life of society.

PART ONE

ELDERS TODAY AND TOMORROW

Elders Are Growing
in Numbers

A new situation is emerging in the United States and Canada: an unprecedented throng of men and women, steadily increasing in both real and proportional numbers, are living long beyond the ages of parenthood and remunerative employment.

Every day 5,000 persons in the United States turn 65 and 3,600 who are 65 or older die — a daily net gain of 1,400 in the older segment of the population. This point has been reached through steady growth:

- In 1900 3 million persons 65 and older comprised 4 percent of the U.S. population.
- By 1980 the number of elders had increased eightfold, reaching 25 million or 11 percent of the total.
- By 2000 it is projected that there will be 32 million older Americans — 12 percent of the population.[1]

The older population of Canada has also grown consistently:

- In 1901 250,000 men and women 65 and older were 5 percent of the Canadian population.
- By 1981 a nearly tenfold growth brought the figures to 2.4 million and 9.7 percent.
- By 2001 the projected figures are approximately 12 million and 12 percent.[2]

The most dramatic phenomenon will occur in the older age-groups in the second decade of the twenty-first century. This will be the result of the post–World War II "baby boom," the sharp increase in birthrates after 1945. During the twenty-year period from 1946 to 1965, 77 million persons were born in the United States. That was 70 percent more than had been born during the previous twenty years. In terms of percentages, the baby-boom generation's size is even more strongly accented because the generation following it — persons born in the later part of the 1960s and in the 1970s—is much smaller as a result of declining birthrates during those years. The same "baby-boom" and "baby-bust" trends characterized Canada's population during those years.

Elementary and secondary schools, and now colleges and universities, have been forced to face up to the dramatic expansion and contraction of their constituencies. So have church schools and youth programs, businesses, the health professions, and governmental and voluntary agencies.

The baby-boom generation in both the United States and Canada will begin turning 65 in the year 2011. There will be far more elders than ever before, in both absolute and relative terms. From 2011 to 2025 the population segment 65 and older in the United States will increase by more than 1 million people each year. Canada will experience a comparable growth.

Projections concerning the older population can be made with reasonable certainty because all the people who will be 65 or older through the year 2050 have already been born. Projections could be affected, to be sure, by migration, scientific breakthroughs, or natural disasters; they also could be drastically altered by an ecological catastrophe, nuclear war, or even a so-called conventional war.

This study is addressed to the church. Although the writer is from the Lutheran Church in America (LCA), it is hoped that the study is applicable to other churches as well. It seeks to highlight some of the implications for the churches of the demographic revolution that is underway and the changes taking place in older adults themselves. Although the LCA has never secured information on the age composition of its congregations,[3] it is likely that elders comprise a higher percentage of the membership of most church bodies than of the total population of both the United States and Canada. In terms of sheer numbers older men and women are a major group within the community of faith. We also must look, however, at what older people are like today and ponder what they may be like tomorrow.

Elders Are People of
Rich Diversity

Older adults, as a group, exhibit more differences among themselves than are found in any other segment of the population. Although most individuals remain basically the same throughout life, they do become more unlike one another as they grow older. The elderly vary in background and experience, racial and ethnic characteristics, abilities and disabilities, family relationships and social status, income and health, interests and attitudes. Countless decisions of a lifetime have gone far to determine what people are now like. Some have yielded repeatedly to outside pressures and have allowed the social stereotypes of aging to become self-fulfilling prophecies for them. Others have demonstrated strong commitments that enable them to maintain independence; they refuse to allow the negative attitudes of others to turn them from their course.

Elders are a people of rich diversity. Each man or woman ages in unique ways at a unique pace; within each one different functions change at different rates. The deepest need of every older adult — and of every other human being — is to be valued as a *person* within a network of distinctive and worthwhile relationships.

They Are "Young-Old" and "Old-Old"

There are more than one generation in the older years. Bernice L. Neugarten now of Northwestern University had identified two broad groups: the "young-old," roughly ages 55–75, and the "old-old," roughly above 75.[4] The distinction is based not so much on chronological age as on social, psychological, and health characteristics.

The young-old are relatively healthy and vigorous, relatively affluent (in comparison with the old-old), relatively free from the traditional responsibilities of work and younger family, and better educated than elders of an earlier time. It is a mistake to regard them as having the physical and mental disabilities and social handicaps that often become the lot of the generations above them. An example of this mistake, which encourages demeaning stereotypes, occurred in a news report on the 1983 Assembly of the World Council of Churches, in Vancouver, British Columbia. The last two items in a summary list of assembly actions "supported fuller involvement of all groups in church life, especially women, youth and the poor," and "called on churches to become a 'healing and sharing reality' for the disabled, aged and addicted." Older persons belong in the first item just as naturally as "women, youth and the poor." Indeed, most older adults are women, and a disturbing number of them are poor. The arrangement of categories in the two items implies that elders have no other role than to be recipients of service and ignores the fact that they, especially the young-old, are a tremendous resource for the church and the community.

Another example that both reflects and fosters destructive myths concerning age is the prayer in the *Lutheran Book of Worship*, entitled "The Poor and the Neglected":

> Almighty and most merciful God, we call to mind before you all those whom it would be easy to forget: the homeless, the destitute, the sick, *the aged*, and all who have none to care for them. . . . (italics the writer's)[5]

Here "the aged"— and the impression is that this refers to all older adults — are almost automatically included in a litany with "the homeless, the destitute, the sick, . . . and all who have none to care for them." It is simply one more instance of the frequent appearance of the phrase "aged and infirm" in our prayers.

The old-old, of course, do have more serious health problems than the young-old; they require more social services and face more acutely the anticipation of death. Even as the young-old must not be viewed as if in the same situation as their seniors, neither should the old-old be expected to perform with the vigor of those who are younger. Nevertheless, among the old-old there are large numbers who continue to rejoice in physical vitality, mental alertness, and a buoyant spirit.

A new phenomenon is that one out of every three young-old persons has one or both parents living. Thus, just at the time of their retirement, these women and men carry the responsibility for their aging fathers or mothers. Often they are still bearing the financial obligation for the education of their own children.

They Are of All Racial and Ethnic Groups

Although all racial and ethnic groups in the United States have their elders, whites age 65 and older comprise a higher proportion (11.2 percent) of the total white population than that comprised by older members of other groups in their respective total populations. Among blacks the corresponding figure is 7.8 percent; among people of Hispanic origin it is 4.5 percent; among American Indians, Eskimos, and Aleuts it is 5.3 percent; and among Asian and Pacific Islanders it is 6.7 percent. In Canada only 3.5 percent of the "original peoples" are age 65 and older. Their highest proportions are in the Northwest Territories, Quebec, and the Yukon.

Whites are disproportionately represented in the older population of the United States because of their longer life expectancy and also because of their lower birthrate, factors which have the effect of increasing the percentages at the older end of the age scale. It seems likely that whites live longer because, as a group, they usually have healthier living conditions and better access to medical care, and are less poverty-stricken than members of other racial and ethnic groups. This circumstance must be an area for continuing concern and action by the churches.

In recent years the number of nonwhite elders in the United States has been growing more rapidly than the number of white elders. Also, the life-expectancy gap between whites and the others has been consistently narrowing. In 1950 whites could expect to live eight years longer than other Americans. By 1977 this differential had decreased to five years.

Most Elders Are Women

In the days of John Adams and Thomas Jefferson, old age was a man's time. More women died in childbirth than men died in warfare. But the story is different today. The majority of older adults are women; their number is growing twice as fast as the number of older men. The last U.S. census in which men outnumbered women was in 1940. In 1980, though males were still more numerous than females up to age 23, at every age beyond 23 women were in progressively larger majorities. The gap is even more striking after age 85. This pattern is true for older women and men in all racial and ethnic groups, and in both Canada and the United States. Although there has been a preponderance of females in the population, researchers are examining the long-term effects of the increase of cigarette smoking, alcohol use, and stress-producing endeavors among women to see if the tendency is changing.

These demographic changes have important implications for marital status. More than half of all persons 65 or older are married and live in husband-wife households. Nevertheless, since women live longer and men tend to marry women younger than themselves, most older men are married and most older women are widowed.

Older women are often victims of special problems. In both overt and subtle ways they may be demeaned because of their sex. Many of their difficulties in later years — in income, for example — are caused by situations arising in earlier years. They may also be demeaned because of age. If they are members of minority groups, their experiences with sexism and ageism are made worse by the addition of racism.

Elders Are Sexual Beings

A primary element in the individuality and diversity of elders (as of other human beings) is sexuality. Men and women are often capable of sexual activity into their seventies, eighties, and beyond. There may be a "slowing down" in both sexes, and there may be some physiological conditions that are usually treatable, but these changes do not follow the commonly voiced stereotypes. Societal attitudes — shared by older adults themselves — are more decisive than physiological conditions in reducing sexual activity in later life. One can imagine the discouragement to normal sexual enjoyment caused by such epithets as "dirty old man" and "silly old woman," which imply that beyond a certain age it is not proper, or even possible, to engage in sexual activity.

Negative attitudes concerning sex have had an unfortunate influence on many homes for the elderly. Husbands and wives living in separate rooms with little opportunity to be together in privacy, staff opening doors without knocking, nurses reprimanding or even ridiculing residents who express affection by touching each other —

these are a few of the ways in which some nursing homes (not all, by any means) violate the dignity and individuality of elders.

Many older people are blocked from sexual expression by lack of partners. A few are discouraged from establishing new relationships by adult children who are either misguided or are operating from questionable motives. Others are prevented from normal activity by destructive societal myths about sex in the older years.

A large number of elders, to be sure, choose to enjoy a satisfying life without physical sex. This underscores the fact that sexuality means far more than the sex act: it is a fundamental part of living. It encompasses the whole range of relationships between male and female, and involves the totality of the sexual needs of women and men regardless of age.

Elders Are Members of Families

The family is important to older adults; older adults are important to the family. But what is the family? How shall it be defined?

For a long time the churches — as well as society in general — have assumed that the nuclear, or conjugal, family consisting of father, mother, and children is the norm. Churches have organized their programs of education and fellowship on the basis of this assumption. Despite an increasing awareness that a large number of contemporary families are not nuclear, church practice has often implied that persons who are not married or bearing children are atypical, not in the "normal" family setting.

Today there are large numbers of men and women who do not marry, as well as single-parent families, couples who choose not to have children, unmarried couples (including older persons) living together, and people dwelling in group situations. Although all these individuals have reason to object to any bias toward the nuclear structure as the norm, the focus of this study is upon elders and the family.

As long as the churches tend to be oriented toward the two-generation family and, indeed, to concentrate on the family's function in relation to children and young people, older persons will be treated, to some degree, as outsiders in both family and congregational life. Fortunately, there is movement for the better — toward the realization that an adequate view of the family should include elders.

It should be stressed that more than 50 percent of older households consist of two-person, husband-wife family units.

They Find Much Meaning in Family

Whatever their own marital status, older men and women usually find much meaning in "family." One reason is that the family is a

15

vehicle of social and psychological *continuity*. Ties to family members (despite changes that occur in those ties) may be one of the few threads that continue through the years. Elders find they also have much to contribute to the sense of family continuity. They provide a memory that is essential to a deeper understanding of life and its relationships.

A second source of meaning that older adults find in the family is the opportunity for *personal* relationships. Public and private social-service agencies and health-care institutions are sometimes justly criticized for impersonal handling of the problems of elders. But when a family deals with its own older members it usually does so in personal terms, even when relationships are not warm. To be sure, the personal can become demonic in those families in which the elderly are physically, mentally, or emotionally abused. This subject will be dealt with more fully in succeeding sections.

The pervasive belief that the typical U.S. or Canadian family is alienated from and neglects its elders has been exposed as a fallacy by Ethel Shanas and her colleagues. On the basis of twenty-five years of research, Shanas states that families are still serving the major needs of older persons. The proportion of elders having an adult child living within a ten-minute drive (50–60 percent) has remained fairly constant for more than twenty years, as has the proportion seeing at least one of their children in the two days prior to being interviewed for the study (53 percent). Most older people have living brothers or sisters, and one-third of them report having seen at least one sibling in the previous week.[6] A frequently significant personal relationship is that between grandparents and grandchildren.

In extended families help flows in all directions: older parents help their children, and adult children assist their parents. These helping patterns often extend to grandchildren and even great-grandchildren.[7] Older parents may help the younger generations with money, advice, or babysitting services. Adult children may assist their aging parents with home health care, home maintenance, transportation, or money. In many families members who have never married have meaningful associations with nieces, nephews, siblings, and cousins. Family-type relationships often exist where there are no ties of blood or marriage. Godparents, older neighbors, and friends of the family may be significant members of the personalized helping network.

A third source of meaning that older adults find in the family is emotional support through *affection*. The information just cited on the personal interchanges taking place among kin do not speak adequately to the quality of the relationships. Affection is difficult to measure, yet it is likely the most important element of all.[8] Despite the positive aspects of Shanas's research results, the fact remains that a distressing number of elders are deeply lonely. This is indeed an urgent concern of the church.

Changes in the Family Are Affecting Elders

There are changes in the family that limit these potentials. A lower rate of fertility, except during the 1946–65 period, means that many older women and men have fewer adult children with whom to relate and upon whom to depend in time of need. Similar results come from today's persistently mobile society. Young people who move long distances to pursue education or occupations become geographically unavailable for frequent association with their elders, for direct expressions of affection, or for mutual assistance. The negative effects of this mobility may be offset somewhat by improvements in communication and transportation — at least for persons with the financial ability to take advantage of them.

Divorce and remarriage may also change the way that younger and older family members relate to each other. Divorce increases the number of individuals who enter old age without the support and companionship of spouses. Child-custody decisions may cause some elders to lose all or most of their contacts with grandchildren or great-grandchildren. And what about stepfamilies? What are the relationships likely to be among stepgrandparents, stepparents, stepchildren and stepgrandchildren? Never-married family members are also affected by situations of alienation and increased complexity. It is essential that research pursue answers to such perplexing and disturbing questions.

The sharp increase in the number of women employed outside the home has significance for the older years. On the one hand, for today's elders this means that daughters, the traditional "kin keepers" of our culture, have less time and strength for family responsibilities, including the care of vulnerable older family members. One implication of this situation is that sons should enter more actively than they have into the role of kin keeper. For that group of elders who will be able to remain in independent living situations if they receive certain supportive services, where will this help come from if not from their adult children? Will this situation force government to expand its support systems even more than would otherwise be the case? Will or can the churches and voluntary organizations fill the gap? Will reduced availability of adult children compel the enormous multiplication of nursing homes?

On the other hand, this change in the roles of women promises that women who spend substantial portions of their lives in the work force may be different persons when they reach age 65 from the current generation of older women. Greater independence during their earlier years may alter their perceptions of what they should be doing in their later years. They will experience retirement personally rather than indirectly through their husbands. Since they likely will be better off financially than most older women presently are, they will be less dependent on the earnings of their husbands, the good will of relatives, or the public welfare system. It seems likely, however, that the future will see more older women living without a supportive immediate family and separated by distance from siblings.

Some Elders Are Victims of Family Violence

Family violence is a major, though hidden, problem, and elders are among the victims. Beginning in 1982, the Austin, Texas, Gray Panthers conducted a statewide survey of fifteen hundred professionals most likely to encounter elder abuse in their work: physicians, nurses, police officials, justices of the peace, hospital social workers, and others. The survey inquired about the extent of abuse of older people these professionals encountered, what kinds of abuse they observed, and what factors were believed to have contributed to the abuse. Almost two-thirds of the respondents said that they had encountered elder abuse in their work. Some of the findings on those elders who had been abused are as follows:

- 75 percent were victims of exploitation, the improper use or outright theft of the older person's funds or property.
- 72 percent had been verbally or emotionally abused, insulted, threatened, humiliated, or frightened.
- 62 percent suffered physical abuse, ranging from physical restraint to beatings to sexual assault.

- 50 percent had been subject to active neglect, including the withholding of necessities such as food, medicine, money, and bathroom assistance.[9]

One of the problems in finding older people who are abused is that they are isolated much of the time because of illness, lack of transportation, or confinement comparable to imprisonment. It is estimated that only one-tenth of them are identified. The respondents to the survey said that most of the abuse cases can be traced to longstanding problems within their homes: overcrowded living conditions, poverty, marital conflict, difficult tasks imposed by the elder's physical or mental condition, and personality tension among the individuals involved.[10]

A government study summarizing the relatively meager results of research on family violence emphasizes that this tragic phenomenon is a manifestation of a violent society. It also points out evidence that "violence begets violence": each generation learns to be violent by being a participant in a violent family.[11] Obviously, family abuse, whether it affects children, spouses, or elders, is enormously complex.

A Dynamic View of the Family Is Required

What lies in the future? Probably neither the nuclear family nor the extended family as such. Recognizing that there is already great variety in how people organize their family life, sociologists are stressing a dynamic view of the family as "a system of relationships in which the roles and positions of each individual are changing in relation to the actions of other family members upon them."[12] In the context of such a view, differences among generations and individuals can be accepted and conflicts can be used creatively to further the common life of the family and the family's service to the community beyond.

A truly dynamic family, despite present and future changes, can be a source of strength for persons facing the major crises of aging: the death of a spouse or adult child; the experience of becoming dependent upon sons or daughters, usually associated with other transitions that are negative in character; in a minority of cases, institutionalization; and the realization that all these problems are traumatic also for the middle generation of adults who themselves face adjustments to the aging process. Within the setting of a dynamic family, older women and men, including those who have never married or have remained childless, should be able to clarify their roles and life styles in relation to the life styles of family members from other generations. By viewing elders as whole persons who contribute in their own ways to the family's life, the family is in a strategic position to combat the stereotypes of aging that violate and frequently destroy people.

Social institutions, including the church, "wishing to understand and serve older adults within the context of family life, must re-examine their assumptions and value judgments, not limiting their view of the family to procreative and nurturing roles."[13]

Elders Vary in Economic/Financial Circumstances

Adequate Income Means Access

An adequate and secure income is as essential in the older years as at any other stage of life. Although a good financial position by no means assures a trouble-free old age, elders with satisfactory incomes have access to better choices of housing, travel, recreation, medical care, church activity, educational opportunities, and friendships. Older people with inadequate incomes are caught in a demoralizing struggle against poverty and its multiple problems. They may cut back on necessary visits to the doctor and the dentist, eat less-nutritious food, neglect to make repairs to the house, give up the car, and often dwell in loneliness and boredom within their four walls.

Retirement Brings a Drop in Income

"The central economic fact of later life," says James D. Manney, Jr., "is the sharp drop in income that comes with retirement. Once retired, the older person is likely to remain retired. Few will ever again receive significant income from paid employment."[14] Many, perhaps most, of the elderly poor have become poor for the first time after becoming old. Furthermore, because they are on basically fixed incomes and must contend with inflation, most elders are destined to become relatively poorer as the general society's living standards rise.[15]

Social Security (in Canada, Old Age Security/Guaranteed Income Supplement) and private pension checks for persons who retire are much lower than the income paid to men and women still active in the labor force. Although employment and/or investments augment the incomes of some, for the majority of older adults Social Security

21

and OAS/GIS are the most important sources. Private pensions, although growing in importance, still cover only limited numbers of elders.

Thus, in 1979 the median income in the United States of families headed by persons age 65 and over was $11,316, while that for families headed by persons under 65 was $21,201. One-fourth of the families headed by persons 65 and over had incomes below $7,275. Individuals 65 and over who live alone or with relatives are almost invariably in lower financial positions than are families.

Minority-Group Elders, Older Women, and Persons 85 and Over Are the Poorest

One of the most disturbing aspects of the economic situation of older adults in the United States is the tragic plight of aged blacks, Hispanic persons, and American Indians. The incomes of older black families and black individuals average only two-thirds those of older whites, with the situations of older black women the worst of all blacks. The circumstances of elders of Hispanic origin are similar to those of blacks. American Indians, however, appear to be the poorest of all. Though information is scarce, some authorities say that most Native Americans live on less than $800–$1,000 a year.

Many minority-group elderly persons either are not eligible for U.S. Social Security or receive very little from that source. Domestic and farm laborers, a great many of whom are from minority groups, have not been covered until recently. Large numbers of American Indians have worked only sporadically; on some reservations more than half of the work force is unemployed. For too many of these minority-group Americans, old age can mean only increasing dependency, squalor, and depression — mitigated in some cases by warm family ties, a mutual intergenerational sharing of their experiences, and a deeply personal faith in God.

Older women, the majority in every category of elders, are steadily increasing in numbers. As we have seen, most women are widowed by age 70. If they have been employed at all, many have worked in lower-paying jobs and have moved in and out of the labor force while bearing children. Older women in general, therefore, have lower financial resources than do men.[16]

Even more tragically, the oldest members of all societal groups, who are also the most rapidly growing segment of the population 65 and over,[17] are the poorest and neediest of all. The overwhelming majority of them, of course, are women.

Fifteen percent of U.S. elders (3.6 million households) live beneath the government poverty threshold. In addition, substantial numbers are at a level only slightly above that threshold, and, from the standpoint of most of the readers of this study, struggle in poverty.

In this unhappy picture we see the complex effects of institutional racism, sexism, and ageism. These problems are interwoven into the very fabric of our society. Unless that fabric can be mended soon, we are well on our way to becoming permanently divided between rich and poor, white and minority groups, young and old. The church is also part of that fabric.

Social Darwinism, with its emphasis on "the survival of the fittest," is rearing its ugly head in both the United States and Canada. In Canada's current debate on pension reform, some bankers and business leaders are arguing that people should look after themselves and that government has no responsibility for promoting the economic well-being of every citizen. The predicament of the poor and minority-group persons, including the old among them, becomes vastly more difficult in nations that are "gung-ho" on huge expenditures for armaments.[18] And in a situation of major disaster, the elderly, of all people, would be the most expendable.

Christians are challenged to battle for new decisions and actions within the church and, from that base as well as individually, to struggle for justice in community life and public policy. People who are old or poor or black or disabled or sick, or a combination of these, have every right of access to the blessings of a democratic society — under the rubric of justice, not charity. To realize that objective, however, aggressive consciousness-raising and advocacy, focusing on specifics and involving elders themselves, is necessary.

The most effective way for Christians and the church to advocate legislation to enhance the lives of elders is to join with allies — organizations, coalitions, advocacy networks on aging — many of which are in a position to be better informed than the church. The collective approach has a better chance of making an impact upon governmental bodies and the decisions they make concerning income maintenance, housing, health care, transportation, and other vitally important issues.

A final word from William J. Hanna, executive director of the Colorado Congress of Senior Organizations:

> The vision of the aging advocate must extend far beyond merely more services and benefits for older persons. Such a narrow advocacy would itself further segregate the elderly from the rest of society. Our goal as advocates is not simply to seek minimum dependency and maximum independence for the elderly. The goal must be to find ways to affirm and express the interdependence of all. And the missing role of the elder is one of the major deficiencies of our still too age-segregated society.[19]

Many Older Adults Are Not Poor

These disturbing realities should not be allowed to obscure the fact that many older adults are not poor. Although elders are more heavily concentrated on the lower rungs of the economic ladder than are the people under 65, substantial numbers of them have considerable economic means. In 1979, for instance, nearly one-third of all families headed by persons 65 or older had incomes of $15,000 or more, with one-fifth having in excess of $20,000.

During the last two decades the average economic position of older Americans has improved. The change is the result of such factors as automatic annual cost-of-living adjustments in Social Security payments since 1974, previous congressionally mandated increases in Social Security benefits, and growth in the number of persons receiving private pensions.

Will this improvement continue into the future? It is difficult to say because of the strains that will be placed upon Social Security and pension systems and the political decisions that might be made to deal with these strains. Cynthia M. Taeuber of the U.S. Bureau of the Census also suggests that slower job advancement and decline in relative wages in coming years will reduce lifetime earnings. Furthermore, she adds, the working life span of many may be shortened or the lifetime employment pattern may be altered by pressures to move off the job ladder to alternative activities.[20]

Tensions Exist Between Generations in Relation to Social Insurance and Other Benefit Programs

In the United States there is "an implicit social contract whereby a person is willing to pay his or her Social Security taxes now to underwrite the current benefit of a retired person on the assumption and expectation that future generations of workers will be willing to pay for the person when he or she retires (for example) in the year 2000."[21]

In recent years the increase in the size and proportion of older persons, the corresponding decrease in the work force, trends toward earlier retirement, and the effects of inflation are beginning to deepen tensions between younger and older generations. Although these issues, which affect private pensions as well as public programs, are at first economic concerns, they soon move into the arena of public policy and politics. A number of considerations will cast light upon the issues involved.

1. It is not accurate to look only at the dependency ratio between the 65 and older population segment and the working-age segment, ages 18 to 64. Large numbers of children and disabled persons of all ages are also among the beneficiaries. During the period when the number of older persons has been growing, the number of children has been decreasing. The total dependency ratio, reflecting the number of dependent children and dependent elders over against the number of those in the working force, remains fairly steady, with even a slight decline projected for the turn of the century. It is necessary to recognize, however, that the comparison is modified to some extent by the fact that the cost of each younger dependent to society is much less (about one-third) than the cost of each older dependent.[22] These figures do not include the 4.5 million disabled workers and their dependents and survivors who are covered by Social Security in the United States.

2. Most old-age dependency costs in the United States are allocated at the federal level of government, while most of the child dependency costs (mainly educational expenses) are borne by families and local and state levels of government.[23]

3. Although 65 is the age on which most calculations and discussions are based,[24] earlier retirement by many workers has caused a considerable change in the dependency ratio. It is too early to evaluate the influence on this situation of the 1978 increase of mandatory retirement to age 70 in private industry and its elimination altogether in federal employment. Public policy decisions will have to be made concerning positive incentives — such as the availability of good jobs and the continuation of fringe benefits[25] — for interested persons to

work longer. Serious political consideration is likely to be given also to the possible raising of the age at which full retirement benefits are granted.

4. Persons who object to the fact that the Social Security system requires younger and middle-aged workers to support retired elders must face the alternative: they would be in the position of supporting older members of their families solely by means of their own resources. This would not only cost many of them more than social insurance, but it would also be far more demeaning for their seniors and would probably increase tensions between the generations. The same circumstances would also exist when they themselves retire.

Elders Suffer from Myths About Income

Older men and women who are poor are subjected to popular myths about income. Some critics assume that poverty is their own fault, that they were improvident in earlier years. Others suggest that plenty of jobs are available for older persons who wish to work. Still others seem to think that Social Security by itself is an adequate source of income for satisfactory living. Effective refutation of these myths would require more space than is available in this study.[26] Their persistence underscores the existence of demeaning attitudes toward the poor, including the elderly poor — attitudes which have the potential of turning even uglier in debates concerning the distribution of public resources.

Most Elders Are in Reasonably Good Health, but Many Have Multiple Medical Problems

Most Elders Are in Reasonably Good Health

In a recent survey of a large number of relatively well-informed people, most of the respondents guessed that 20 percent of persons age 65 and over are in institutional care at any given time. The correct figure is 4 percent! To be sure, a larger number are in such care at some time, and even 4 percent represents a million people. Nevertheless, the assumption that so many elders are in institutions at any given time reflects a widespread impression that the majority of older adults are characteristically afflicted by poor health. This is an ingredient in the negative image of the aging process and of older people held by a considerable portion of the public.

In addition to the 4 percent, 10–15 percent more elders are able to cope and to live in home and community settings *provided* they are aided by various supportive services. (This will be discussed in a later section.) The remaining majority are living quite normal lives.

Although older adults use physicians and hospitals more than younger people, it is to be stressed that most individuals 65 and older are *not* hospitalized in any given year. Data from a 1979 Health Interview Survey reveal that fewer than two out of every ten older persons were hospitalized in the previous year, compared with one in ten in the under-65 population.

Even among the older men and women who are incapacitated by illness, the often-used term "senile" is devastating and usually inaccurate. There are different kinds of brain syndrome. Some are irreversible, but more are reversible.[27] In the latter cases there have been some remarkable demonstrations of the partial or full recovery of

27

afflicted persons when they have been given appropriate medical care and nutrition and when their interest and motivation have been reawakened by sensitive care givers willing to spend time in the effort. Even in cases of irreversible brain syndromes, medical science can often do much to minimize side problems and enable the ill persons to live reasonably satisfying lives. All too often a patient will respond to the pessimism of the family, the physician, and others in attendance by becoming helpless and hopeless long before his or her actual condition warrants it.

When speaking of the health concerns of older adults, we must walk a tightrope between two essential tasks: (1) counteracting the stereotype that to be old is to be sick and that most older people must be pampered, protected, and cared for; and (2) acknowledging the real medical problems of many elders and emphasizing the urgency of radical revisions of our health systems to deal effectively with those problems.

Many Elders Have Multiple Medical Problems

Over 80 percent of older adults, chiefly in the old-old category, have at least one chronic condition, and multiple conditions are a common occurrence.[28] Nevertheless, fewer than one elder in six say they can no longer carry on normal activities, and only one in five reports some limitation of the amount and kind of usual pursuits. Extremely small proportions of *noninstitutionalized* older persons indicated that they needed help with bathing, dressing, using the toilet, or eating. It is critical to stress that, although the need for these kinds of personal assistance increases with advancing age, the vast majority of elders — even among those 85 and older — continues to perform independently these activities of daily living.

Older adults use health services at a rate far greater than all other adults. Although they represent only 11 percent of the U.S. population, their combined medical costs are about 29 percent of the nation's total expenditure for health care. Physician visits (home and office) increase as patients become older,[29] and the hospitalization rate for elders is two-and-one-half times greater than that of younger persons. They go to the hospital more often, stay longer, and account for 20 percent of total surgical procedures.

Mental illness is a problem among older men and women. It is estimated that about 3 percent of all persons 65 and over live in public or private institutions as a result of mental illness or suffer mental illness as a byproduct of their institutionalization. Most of those affected are age 75 and over. Also, among noninstitutionalized elders perhaps 5 percent are either psychotic or have severe mental disturbances. Others beyond this number have some neurotic or psychiatric problems or personality disorders. A respectable body of psychiatric opinion holds that no individual who manages to function in the community can be considered mentally ill. Despite the imprecision of definitions and surveys in this area, it is clear that attention must be given to the problems of many older people in relation to mental health.[30]

A significant problem among the elderly is suicide. The rate of suicide increases with age and is highest among older white men. This does not necessarily imply depression; other reasons might be loss of status, the desire to protect finances for a surviving spouse, the decision to avoid intense pain, disablement, institutionalization, or lingering death. For nonwhite women and men and for white women, the suicide curve is bell shaped, with the peak during the earlier adult and middle years. Overall, 25 percent of known suicides in the United States take place among the 11 percent of the population who are 65 and over. The actual figure is probably higher, since families, out of shame or guilt, are frequently unwilling to report suicides. Furthermore, these statistics do not include those who have allowed themselves to die passively by such measures as neglecting self-care or not seeking help for severe medical problems.

Poor older people have more health problems than those of higher economic status. Older single persons are more frequently malnourished and lack the emotional support that is so important in preventing and recovering from disease. Blacks and members of other minority groups have higher death rates than whites, as well as much higher rates of diseases such as cancer and diabetes. Their health problems are often associated with lower income and factors such as inadequate housing, greater exposure to danger, and poor sanitation—all of which accompany low income.[31] It is significant, however, that once blacks reach old age, their death rates are lower than those of whites. Evidently, only the toughest have survived into old age.

Chemical misuse, abuse, and dependency is another serious health problem among older adults. A conservative estimate is that the number of older problem drinkers in the United States exceeds one million persons.[32] Furthermore, in an effort to get relief from pain, tension, or illness at minimal cost, elders often buy over-the-counter drugs in addition to prescription medicines. Some take drugs intended for other people, or they take old and new prescriptions together. Some find it difficult to keep track of the assigned doses, with the result that they take too much or too little or get medicines confused. We hear that old men and women in nursing homes are frequently given drugs to keep them passive. And, unfortunately, there are physicians who find it easier to give pills than to listen to complaints, diagnose carefully, and work out effective treatment plans. The dangers of all of these abuses are multiplied by the perils of combining different drugs, including alcohol. Physicians, pharmacists, nurses, families, and elders themselves must be informed and on guard against chemical misuse, abuse, and dependency.

Health Care and Social Service Systems
Need to Be Examined

Needless to say, the aging of America puts a tremendous strain on the health-care system. The achievements of that system are the major reason for the amazing extension in life expectancy and the increase in the number of people living into the older years. The achievement, however, now presents growing problems that the health and social service systems did not fully anticipate and are not fully organized to provide for. What are some of those problems?

1. Elders often receive services that are not appropriate while many of their basic needs go unattended. Their physical illnesses are accompanied by and exacerbated by social, psychological, and economic impairments that frequently are not dealt with. A health system that focuses on the curing of acute infections and diseases, and is usually organized according to organ or disease specialties, is poorly equipped to treat women and men who have multiple diagnoses and suffer from ailments of mind and spirit that can be understood only in terms of the whole person.

2. Medical personnel are often influenced by stereotypic attitudes toward the afflictions of elders, and, therefore, they often have a low

motivation to deal with them. What do you expect at your age? is a question all-too-frequently addressed by physicians to older men and women complaining of illness or aches and pains. Doctors trained to work for cures of acute illnesses are often not inclined to give the time necessary to treat a person with a cluster of chronic medical problems. In one study fifteen hundred general practitioners and internists were asked to classify a number of conditions occurring frequently among elders as either conditions that are normal or that are caused by disease. The results showed that many physicians tend to dismiss many *treatable* disease-related conditions as if they are expected accompaniments of old age. For example, between one-half and three-fourths of the physicians incorrectly classified senile cataracts, cerebral arteriosclerosis, retinal arteriosclerosis, senility, and enlarged prostate as belonging to the aging process. Such errors suggest that these physicians may fail to treat conditions that can be corrected.[33]

3. The health system has a bias toward institutional care of the elderly. This is certainly true of Medicare and Medicaid in the United States. A study by the Department of Health, Education, and Welfare (now the Department of Health and Human Services) indicated that 14–25 percent of institutionalized elders may not *need* institutional care. Yet in 1976 only about 1 percent of more than $3 billion in Medicaid funds used for persons age 65 and over was spent on home care. The greatest amount by far was used for care in intermediate and skilled-care nursing homes.

Dr. Lewis Thomas of the Memorial Sloan-Kettering Cancer Center in New York City spoke bluntly when he called nursing homes "halfway technologies" because they treat the manifestations of disease instead of its mechanisms. Thomas said that the iron lung was a halfway technology in the war against polio. Fortunately, it was replaced by vaccines that struck at the heart of the disease. Therefore, according to Thomas, nursing homes are the equivalent of iron lungs for the dependent elderly, "expensive relics of the days before we found more satisfactory answers to the challenges of human longevity."[34]

It is inevitable that our nations will require more and better nursing homes, but perhaps Dr. Thomas's statement will shock us into searching for a better-balanced approach to health care for older adults. U.S. Senator Alan Cranston declares, "We cannot afford to begin the twenty-first century with a mushrooming population of dependent old people who are no better able to care for themselves than many who are in nursing homes today."[35]

Positive Approaches to Health Care
Must Be Taken Seriously

We do need nursing homes. They are essential links in the continuum of health-care services for elders. These facilities provide intermediate or skilled nursing care for men and women whose overall physical and/or mental condition has declined to the point where previous living arrangements and family or community resources are no longer adequate to meet present needs. Nursing homes are also increasingly components of complexes that include apartment communities, cottages, and other parts of a selection of facilities used by elders at different stages of health.[36]

Society and the church, however, must devote far more concentrated attention to preventive health care, which should not be left entirely to the initiative of the individuals themselves and which should be covered adequately by insurance. There should be a serious emphasis upon home health care, nutrition education, guided exercise, and informed self-help among older persons. There should be intensified efforts to provide a battery of supportive services, most of them nonmedical, that will enable more elders to continue living in their own homes or communities: home visitation, telephone reassurance, respite care, transportation, grocery shopping, limited chore services, home-delivered meals, and so on.

These various positive approaches to health care are to be found under the auspices of community organizations, church/synagogue coalitions, social mission agencies, homes for the elderly, and, often, local congregations. They are not to be seen merely as "alternatives to institutionalization." They are themselves viable options, and are preferred except when a nursing home is the only facility where proper care can be given.

Older adults — and all others, too — will be served best by support systems that assist in the coordination of personal and family health services; take cognizance of social, psychological, and economic factors; and assure independent living insofar as possible.

Living Arrangements Are of Urgent Importance to Elders

"Home" Is the Significant Element

The concept of "home" means warmth and hospitality, independence and safety, privacy and freedom. Unfortunately, far too many older women and men live in situations that others would not consider worthy of the name "home": crowded inner-city flats, remote backwoods shacks, institutions. Although the persons living in these places might choose to call them home, the rest of society, including churches, must be concerned to ensure that elders have living arrangements that meet the fundamental needs for independence, security, identity, and well-being.

When we consider the significance of home, it is not hard to understand why older adults often resist moving, even from what appear to others to be undesirable quarters. A move would put them in unfamiliar surroundings and, most likely, among total strangers. If the move is to an institution, both the prospect and the actual move may be a crushing experience, calling for sensitive efforts to provide understanding and support. Factors essential to satisfactory living arrangements include housing characterized by quality, cost, and location appropriate to individual needs; convenient transportation; and accessibility to private and public resources that assist and enhance daily living.

Since over one-fifth of all U.S. households — some 16 million — are headed by persons age 65 and over, the living arrangements of elders are a national concern.

It Is Often Difficult to Maintain the House

The first basic housing problem of many elders is that they have serious problems continuing to live in homes where they may have been for years. About 70 percent of older household heads own their own homes, and 84 percent of these are mortgage-free. Nevertheless, total housing costs remain high.[37] Although in absolute monetary terms elders spend less on housing than do younger persons, their lower incomes cause them to spend higher proportions of income. Pre–World War II houses, in which more than half of elders live, are often too large for present needs and are difficult to maintain. Most houses, whether old or new, are not built with elders in mind (particularly those elders who are failing physically). There are too many steps; cupboards are too high; bathrooms have slippery floors and lack bars for support; windows are hard to open and close; heating, lighting, and ventilation are inadequate; and doors are too narrow to permit the moving of beds. A large amount of substandard housing is occupied by poor older households, especially by (in order of residence) Hispanic males living alone, black males living alone, families headed by black females, and black females or white males living alone.

Approximately one-third of all elders who are household heads live in rental housing. Because older renters tend to have lower incomes than older homeowners, they spend an even higher proportion of income on housing costs and often have serious difficulty keeping up with steadily rising rents. More than 1.3 million persons age 65 and over receive some form of assistance from the U.S. government's major housing programs.

Older persons living in rental or subsidized housing often have problems getting necessary repairs or utilities such as fuel. Fear of reprisal sometimes keeps them from reporting the problems. One eighty-three-year-old woman in subsidized housing would not report a need for exterminating service in her building because, as she said, "They will put me out, and where would I go?"

More Housing Is Required by Elders

The second basic housing problem of elders is that the supply of living arrangements appropriate for them is severely restricted. Single-family homes within their income levels are hard to find and buy, and condominiums are beyond the financial range of all but a relatively affluent minority. Many have been forced to move from apartments because conversion of the apartments to condominiums has priced those quarters beyond their means. Some turn to mobile-home developments, many of which are very vital communities. Most retirement communities are unavailable to elders who are of limited means or of minority groups. Despite several creative experiments, including some by churches, there is very little "congregate" or group housing that would provide the frail, modest-income elderly with an alternative to completely independent living or placement — often inappropriate — in a long-term care facility. Public housing, already insufficient in supply and quality, is not very reliable in view of the U.S. government's vacillating commitment. Once again, the rich and the well-to-do have their choice of living arrangements, the middle-income people are reasonably comfortable, and the poor exist in inadequate, often crowded, unsafe, and unhealthful housing.

Transportation Helps Older Adults to Participate

Transportation links the homes of elders with the community beyond. It provides access to work opportunities, recreational facilities, church and cultural activities, banks and stores and physicians, family and friends, and social services. William R. Hutton, executive director of the National Council of Senior Citizens, stated before a congressional committee: "Being without transportation is like having a modern kitchen with all the latest appliances and no electricity." Because of the dominance of the private automobile, which many older persons (especially women) cannot afford or are not able to drive, as well as the inadequacy of public transportation in most areas, many older people become virtual prisoners in their homes or immediate neighborhoods. No wonder the 1971 White House Conference on Aging listed transportation as a top priority for older Americans.

Residential Mobility and Family Mobility Are Factors in Life Satisfaction

Despite the much-publicized migration to the Sunbelt, older people in general are less mobile than younger people. It was the young who years ago left the rural areas and moved into the cities to take over new jobs created by industrial development. Again, following World War II, it was younger families, chiefly white, who left the central cities and populated the burgeoning suburbs. Elders tended to remain in the rural communities and the inner cities. Today those "young people" in the suburbs are becoming the new elders, and are facing some of the same circumstances there as their parents faced in the cities.[38]

The mobility of younger generations has caused geographical separation from parental families and the establishment of independent residences. Consequently, the extended family has been replaced by the nuclear family and other kinds of family patterns. Although in a large number of cases the children have not experienced upward mobility, many younger persons have moved into more glamorous, better-paying jobs than the ones held by their parents. This has often led to a social and intellectual separation of generations.[39]

There has been significant population movement among different regions. Between 1970 and 1980, 90 percent of the net U.S. population growth occurred in southern and western states; more than half of the population now lives in those areas. Although a considerable number of people moving to states like California, Florida, and Texas are retired persons, the majority are younger. In the future, however, they, too, will be elders.

Still another change now underway is revealed in the 1980 U.S. census: a one-hundred-fifty-year trend has been broken, as nonmetropolitan areas grew faster (15 percent) than metropolitan areas (9.5 percent). This nonmetropolitan growth is almost entirely in non-farm areas; it has been caused by exurban development, less-expensive housing, relocation of retired persons, and new employment opportunities created as industry has gone into the country. All this presents the church with increasing challenges to reach into less densely settled areas and to deal with individuals and families who prefer to live in smaller communities. Presumably the majority of people making this kind of move are younger families, but in due time they also will be older adults.

The chief losers of population in this migration, of course, are larger metropolitan areas, all but two of them in the North. A large number of older Americans of all nationalities and racial and ethnic groups still live in these cities and their nearer suburbs. There is danger of the proliferation of ghetto situations, as these concentrations of elders are restricted to certain areas by economic pressures or social discrimination. These developments pose at least two challenges to the church: (1) the challenge to join actively in struggles against injustice and for the enhancement of community living; and (2) the challenge to seek out older women and men and include them in the life and ministry of the church, both through the evangelism outreach of existing congregations and through the formation of new congregations.

Elders of Tomorrow
Will Be Different

They Will Be Better Educated

The older adults of the early 1980s still have less formal education than do younger people. We have gone through an era that has seen steadily higher levels of education for all youth. This has been paralleled by vocational training for workers in newly developing industries. Since most of these efforts have targeted the young, the young have had opportunities to acquire more and better education than their elders. A major consequence has been an inversion of status: older women and men — formerly revered partly because of their superior knowledge — more recently have had to rely on their children to translate communications from the complex outside world.

Dramatic changes, however, are already in progress. They will come to fruition as the baby boomers march into the older years. Landon Jones[40] shows the striking contrast between today and tomorrow in educational attainment:

1980s Cohort 65 and Over	*Baby Boomers When 65 and Over*
50 percent — no high school	
34 percent — high school graduates	90 percent — high school graduates
17 percent — one year of college	
10 percent — college graduates (nearly all men)	27 percent — men college graduates
	20 percent — women college graduates

This emerging situation sharpens the challenge to provide increasingly substantial educational opportunities to elders and about elders. First, this should include provision of education for its own sake — history, language, religion, art, music, literature, science. The

Senior Center Humanities Program of the National Council on the Aging is a step in the right direction. So are the AARP Institute of Lifetime Learning, the rapidly expanding ELDERHOSTEL Program, and the efforts of many colleges and universities — including Lutheran institutions — to make college-level courses available to people of all ages. In addition, there are many valuable continuing-education programs provided in communities across both the United States and Canada.

Second, there should be an increase in educational efforts to prepare men and women for retirement, preferably at ages early enough to allow time for planning. Effective preparation will include such topics as constructive attitudes toward aging and retirement; cooperative planning involving husband, wife, and perhaps other relatives and dependents; financial concerns; the making of wills; housing and location; health; and constructive use of time and talent.

Third, there should be education that trains older people for special skills and keeps them up-to-date amid rapid social changes. This may call for reeducation to enter new fields, second careers, or significant volunteer endeavors.

Fourth, there should be more serious education of persons who will work with older adults, both the older adults who are hale and hearty and those who are frail. Professionals and their helpers in medical care and social service, and also volunteers in community programs and institutions need thorough training. Ministers must be schooled in understanding the aging process and the problems and the potentials of elders as well as in guiding a dynamic congregational ministry that enhances the dignity and meets the deepest needs of older people within the context of the total community of faith.

Fifth, intensive efforts should be made to bring the concept of the full life cycle into the education of children and young people.[41] This can include not only some radical changes in curriculum material but also vital intergenerational relationships and participation of resourceful older persons in the education of youth. The changes now taking place in the educational attainments of elders have enormous implications. They are bound to affect attitudes and actions throughout society, and certainly throughout the church. We must pray that leaders in both these realms do not allow themselves to be caught unprepared.

Elders Will Be Increasingly Active in Employment and in Volunteer Activities

Large numbers of older men and women have demonstrated that they can continue in active employment far beyond age 65, if they so choose. When they are unable to do this, the reason may have nothing to do with age. It could be illness or lack of ability. Some people are ineffective workers long before they reach age 65. And some just prefer to stop working as early as possible. The point is that the capacity to work is not simply a matter of age. U.S. Department of Labor studies indicate that older workers (unless ill, injured, or handicapped) do not lack physical steadiness of body, arm, and hand; they have better attendance records at work than do younger persons; they have fewer disabling injuries; and they are more dependable and efficient.

More and more people are launching second careers around ages 50–55. Some are bored and desire a change. Some have felt themselves under too great pressure. Others have sought the excitement of a fresh start. Some have retired early either from personal choice or employer initiative. Many second careers are in the ordained ministry and other church positions. Others are in service fields like social work and community leadership.

An interesting prospect regarding work opportunities for elders is suggested by Cynthia M. Taeuber of the U.S. Bureau of the Census. She anticipates that, because of the smaller size of the young-adult group currently age 18–24, the rate of increase in the total work force will slow down as we approach 1990 to the lowest growth rate in thirty years. One consequence of this is likely to be a more favorable climate for the employment of elders. In fact, many companies requiring skilled workers are beginning their own training programs, not only for young people just out of high school but also for retirees over 55.[42]

In March 1981 Morrison H. Beach, retired chairman of the board of The Travelers Insurance Company, gave a stirring address to the National Council on the Aging on "Business and the Graying of America." He argued that business should open up opportunities for useful, gainful work to the many older people who want to work. Not all but many are able. They have good-to-excellent health and are mentally sharp, skilled, and knowledgeable. They are capable of learning new things. The rewards of such employment would be both psychological and economic: elders would enjoy worthwhile work; business would tap a vast reservoir of talent and experience; and the nation could help improve the gross national product by almost 4 percent over the next twenty-five years and add $40 billion to federal, state, and local tax revenues. Beach advocated lowering barriers on job choice for elders; basing hiring not on age but on skill, ability, and aptitude; and regular provision of "lifetime" planning programs.

"I believe," Beach declared, "that the maturing of America's population is a potential blessing, not a burden. It means that America's quotient of wisdom, experience and stability is about to grow. Of course, there will be problems. But it has always been the genius of Americans to view problems as opportunities."[43]

This is a forward-looking challenge from a leading businessman to the business world. What does the challenge say to the church?

Beach mentioned that Travelers uses retirees to fill temporary jobs in the company instead of turning to temporary service agencies. It also regularly surveys all departments to create job opportunities for more permanent but part-time work. A Travelers' retiree job bank has been set up. This company has moved beyond the old limiting notion of full-time work followed by full-time retirement.

Control Data Corporation is another business that provides special work opportunities. It designates a certain percentage of its jobs for "special workers," for the elderly and women who want to work part time, or for workers in a plant in prison. If a recession comes the company lays off the special workers first, thus protecting the jobs of its regular workers. This example recognizes that in bad times the possibility of hiring older employees is reduced.

Not all retirement activity of older women and men will or should be remunerative employment. The largest amount of it will be volunteer service. The opportunities are endless. Indeed, older volunteers may have even more opportunities today because larger numbers of women, the traditional volunteers, are in the work force. But it is essential that volunteer work in communities and in churches be well organized and competently administered. Those who organize volunteers must sensitively and diligently recruit, train, assign, supervise, and recognize them. They must realize that some people wish only routine work, but others prefer work that uses their experiences, intelligence, and skills. For example, I have a friend who retired after a significant business career. When he volunteered for service with the local American Red Cross chapter, and the leaders learned about his background, he soon became a member of its board of directors and chairman of its personnel committee. In this position he has been presiding over a needed revision of the organization's personnel policies.

A problem faced by older men and women is the work ethic, the concept that puts a premium on achievement and productivity and derives a person's value from his or her work, particularly paid employment. Although it is slowly fading in appeal, the work ethic continues to exert a powerful influence on society and on a large number of individuals, including many who are older. It encourages the idea that retirement transforms one into a nonperson, a drone who does not sting and makes no contribution to the community. Likely, it also causes some retirees to shun volunteer activity in favor of an often-futile search for employment. This often-devastating concept of the work ethic must be counteracted by an emphasis on God's creative and redeeming love as giving dignity to all human beings, regardless of age, circumstance, or activity, and on the significance of every stage of life from birth to death.

We have artificially divided life into three separate parts: education (childhood and youth), the work and child-nurturing years (young adulthood and middle age), and retirement (young-old and old-old). All the way through we have made a sharp distinction between work and leisure. Would not more constructive living result from a creative intermingling of work, leisure, and education throughout the span? There are indications that American society is moving in this direction.[44] Freed from the tyranny of the work ethic and the restrictions of the working day, elders have the opportunity to be pioneers of a new life style.

They Will Be More Politically Involved

Many politicians are becoming aware of the voting power — based on sheer numbers alone — of older people. But most politicians do not yet view this power in partisan terms. So far they feel they can take care of what they envision as "elder concerns" in noncontroversial and low-priority ways. Their attitude resembles the attitude of television stations toward the "public service" programs they are required by law to air. The typical government approach toward the elderly at the present time is probably no more perceptive than the following statement in the *Canada Handbook* introducing its report on the increase of elders in that nation: "The changing proportion of the population in the group aged 65 years and over is of particular interest to those planning facilities for the care of the elderly and determining future pension needs."[45] Facilities for care and pension needs! Is that all that is to be said about a segment of the population during nearly one-third of its life?

This attitude will, of course, change whether or not keener insights emerge spontaneously in the halls of government. It will change not only because the number of older adults is growing rapidly but also because older adults are becoming more sophisticated in the political world. Such recent phenomena as the civil rights movement, the women's movement, and the peace movement, in all of which many of today's elders have taken part, have stimulated a new assertiveness by older people on behalf of their own rights and needs. Although their political objectives and techniques may differ greatly, the Gray Panthers, the American Association of Retired Persons, the National Council of Senior Citizens, the National Caucus on the Black Aged, and various other groups in the United States and Canada have been making a growing impact on political circles. Some of them fight chiefly for governmental action that will benefit elders. The Gray Panthers, however, who deliberately include all ages in their membership, also concentrate their efforts on advancing justice for *all* people, not only elders. This approach is sound.

Political scientists say that no real "aging vote" exists among the contemporary crop of the "young-old," and that such cohesiveness is not likely to emerge very soon, if ever. According to Robert H. Binstock, a substantial portion of older women and men (40–65 percent) do not perceive themselves as old or aged and do not see their grievances as age related. Even comparatively disadvantaged elders do not see their problems of income, health, housing, safety, and transportation as caused solely by age. They see these problems in other contexts as well. Elders identify themselves more strongly in terms of family, educational background, ethnicity, occupation, income, and residence than in terms of age as such. On most public questions the attitudinal differences *between* age groups are far less impressive than those *within* age groups. To be sure, the experience of common retirement status for twenty-five or thirty years could change some of this, and this change could be heightened by political controversies over the distribution of resources according to age or work status.[46]

The implication is that elders view themselves more as members of the body politic or of various subgroups than as members of older generations. It is to be hoped that this means that their numbers, voting strength, and political skills will be directed toward the well-being and fulfilment of all people, especially those of whatever age, race, or class who are the most deprived.

They Will Be More Assertive

Elders of the future will be more assertive in all of life. Signs of this are clear among the current older population. They will not quietly accept the "put-downs," the ageism, and the discrimination common in many situations.[47] The elders of the future — and more and more those in the present — will not wait "hat in hand" for benevolent younger groups to bestow gifts from their bounty. Older persons will expect to take their share of leadership and to participate actively in making the decisions that affect their lives and the good of the general community.

It is true, of course, that there are large numbers of elders who are not self-generating; they never were. They will not move in the directions we envision, and they should not be forced to. However, a new mood is coming over the most alert and aggressive of older adults, particularly but not exclusively among the young-old. They have an enormous potential to be agents of social change in creating an age-irrelevant society, defined by Bernice Neugarten as a society "in which arbitrary constraints based on chronological age are removed and in which all individuals, whether young or old, have opportunities consonant with their needs, desires and abilities."

Professor Neugarten points to the possibility of an exciting future when she writes of the young-old: "If they create an attractive image of aging, thus allaying the fears of the young about growing old, and if they help to eradicate those age norms which are currently meaningless and those age attitudes which are currently divisive, they will do the society an untold service."[48]

A Consistent Philosophy of Aging Is Needed

It is obvious that two incompatible images of the older years exist side by side. One equates that period of life with economic dependency, physical and intellectual decline, and personal isolation. This is the image that fosters the negative stereotypes of aging which this study seeks to combat. It is also the image on which most public policy, most church policy, and most of the "aging industry" are based.

The second image is the one we have been articulating—that of a large number of older adults as energetic, sexually active, increasingly assertive, and capable of involvement in the mainstream. This view interprets the problems of most elders not primarily as "needs" arising from disabilities that naturally accompany aging, but as the denial of opportunity and choice arising from the ageism of a society that devalues its old.

The inconsistency is clear when we observe the major "aging" organizations referred to earlier espousing, on the one hand, the positive, anti-ageist image of older people and, on the other hand, working for legislation based on the negative image of age-related dependency and need. Douglas Nelson describes the confusion of emphases as simultaneously characterizing elders as "dependent-independent; appropriately retired-inappropriately excluded from work; isolated-involved; frail-vital; impoverished-affluent; deserving of special status-subject to arbitrary discrimination; ill-well; and so on."[49]

How shall we resolve the dilemma and arrive at a consensus that will lead to the well-being of elders and all of society? Shall we commit ourselves to Professor Neugarten's concept of the age-irrelevant society? This idea, translated into policy based on need rather than age, has much to be said for it. It can claim growing support in social and physiological research; it harmonizes with significant themes in the "aging movement"; and it may lead to those social changes that best conform to both the personal interest of most older people and the general public interest. This is especially true when applied to the middle-aged and the young-old. The danger is that this approach could be misused by some as an excuse to dismantle the income, health, and social-support programs on which most of the current generation of elders depend absolutely.

Shall we, therefore, update old age, change the public-policy threshold from 65 to 75? There are too few important age-determined characteristics to justify differentiating persons age 60–70 from those age 45–60. It is appropriate, however, to single out the older group (75 and over) for special attention. In policy matters it might be just as valid to make age 75 a transition point from middle to old age as to make age 18 the transition point from youth to adulthood. If it ever becomes public policy to focus services on the 75 and over elders, it would be essential to provide them in the context of the positive image of the older years.

Nelson discusses these policy options more fully in his article. He also poses a third option, the idea of "veteranship." This would correlate age with a distinct social status. It would define elders as veterans of life—"not as a class set apart by like needs and interests, but rather as a heterogeneous community of citizens who have in common the fact that each individual has spent most of a human lifetime experiencing, shaping, and being shaped by the same social history as his/her cohorts." Under the veteranship idea, "programs and policies designed to assure economic security, to permit retirement, to provide specialized social and recreational opportunities, to guarantee adequate health care, to promote age respect and deference are not justified simply on the ground of need *per se*: rather, they are defensible as *earned* entitlements."

The veteranship concept, like all others, has flaws. One is that it would encourage further excesses by some elders who selfishly assert their rights and demand special discounts and privileged treatment—favors that may be unrelated to their actual health or financial circumstances—solely on the basis of age. A second flaw is that, however honorable its intention, veteranship might actually be an invitation to patronize and thus devalue older men and women. In effect, it could parallel certain historical idealizations and devaluations of women. A third flaw is that veteranship might increase the danger of conflict between old and young, especially when applied to the distribution of inadequate national resources.

These are questions that must be thoroughly examined as an essential step in building a viable philosophy with regard to aging and the older adult. Nelson concludes with these words: "Ultimately the value and benefit of advocacy for the elderly lies in the quality and character of the changed social order it helps to create. Defining that new order remains the most pressing and immediate challenge facing the aging movement."

Elders today and tomorrow. They are a changed and changing group of people. The church must take them seriously in new and creative ways. No longer will it suffice to "be nice to the old folks over in the corner." No longer will it be adequate primarily to build nursing homes and retirement communities. Health and social services there must be, of the highest quality and most appropriate kinds, for the frail and vulnerable elderly. Indeed, special efforts must be made to make services available to the poor and those who are members of racial and ethnic minority groups.

The church, however, continually needs to take a good clear look at *all* the elders in its midst, recognize the human resources to be found among the majority of older men and women, and prepare to involve them, not in "playpen activities" or peripheral responsibilities but in the most central expressions of mission.

PART TWO

THE CHURCH'S
RESPONSE

The Call to Respond

A revolution is in progress. It is not marked by the crackle of gun-fire, the crash of bombs, or the rhythm of marching feet. It is a quiet revolution, but it is also profound, because it is working a basic change in the composition of the populations of the United States and Canada and of the constituency of the LCA and other major denomi-nations. The church dare not be caught unprepared; it must respond positively and intelligently to the *demographic revolution.*

The church must also respond to the *changing character* of the elders of today and tomorrow as they interact with their changing social situations. It must deal with the ageism that unimaginatively lumps older men and women into a homogeneous mass; the aliena-tion of some of them from the family and other primary relation-ships; the economic, health, and living-arrangements problems of some of them; and the myths that imply that all older adults are bur-dened with crushing problems, and that, indeed, old age is itself "a problem."

Most deeply and urgently of all, however, the church must respond faithfully to its own *theological imperatives.* The LCA Social State-ment (1978), "Aging and the Older Adult," declares that:

> God's love for all persons is creative and unconditional. Human beings have dignity not because they have achieved success or the esteem of the world, but because they are made in the image of God. They are given the capacity to relate to God in responsible freedom.[1]

The "image of God" is not a human attainment; it is a gift. Value has been placed on us by the Creator, regardless of age, sex, or any other temporal category. This means that it is heresy to hold that "man is man or woman is woman only so long as he or she can pro-duce children or make things. The final conclusion of such an assumption is that people become things that can be discarded when they no longer have full productive power."[2]

The Christian faith sees all human beings as sinners in rebellion

50

against God, and proclaims that in Jesus Christ God has provided redemption for all. In relation to age, redemption requires that we come to terms with mortality and everything else that limits life on this earth. As we are led by the Holy Spirit to perceive our finitude, we are enabled to live with unfinished projects and unanswered questions, to accept our own aging, and to acknowledge death as real and certain. We worry less about "time running out" and rejoice rather in the preciousness of the time remaining. Redemption affirms that, in Christ, God has taken those whom others call "nobodies" or "nonpersons" and made them "new creations," somebodies. The 1978 LCA Social Statement says that in the light of Christian faith, "life is a gift of God, and aging is a natural part of living."

Christians of all ages are members of the body of Christ, the universal priesthood, the holy catholic church. Whether they are clergy or laity, older women and men are in no sense exceptions to this membership — they are fully included in the ministry of God's people in the world. Like all other Christians, they are both receivers and givers in this ministry. They are called to join actively in worship, education, and nurture; to provide leadership in accordance with talents, strength, and interest; to help serve the needs of other people; to labor for justice and human fulfillment; and to share in building up the church for service to the world. They are called to *be the church* wherever they are, whatever they do.

Beyond these components of ministry that they have in common with all believers, elders are the stewards of insights and opportunities for ministry that only they are likely to possess. Out of their experience of the years, most of them are capable of interpreting to younger generations the defeats and victories, sorrows and joys that belong to human life.

Unless they betray their stewardship by aping the young, older adults can help free others from "the belief that frenetic activity is the measure of life . . . and bear witness to the undiminished worth that God attaches to life itself."[3] Furthermore, as persons relatively unobligated to employers, restrictive family traditions, or the arbiters of social status, they can speak out and work on behalf of justice for all people. Maggie Kuhn persistently reminds her peers: "We have nothing to lose!" Finally, elders living in faith can demonstrate the power of the gospel as it sheds the light of the resurrection upon failing capacities, losses, severed relationships, and death itself.

"Aging and the Older Adult"

The carefully chosen words of the title of the 1978 LCA Social Statement stress that this church's interest and action in this connection should have two foci: aging and the older adult. On the one hand, there should be a focus on "the older adult," on the particular group of people who have reached the later years of life. On the other hand, there should be a focus on "aging," the natural process that characterizes all human beings throughout their lives.

Older adults are of special importance to the church for reasons other than numbers or percentages. Dr. David O. Moberg of Marquette University tells us that research indicates that "in nearly all communities more older people are members of churches and other religious bodies than of any other type of voluntary social organization." Older people may not be as *active* participants in church worship and life as are the middle-aged. This is probably because of factors such as physical disability, lack of transportation, financial embarrassment, or the sense of being left out. But there is evidence, according to Dr. Moberg, that internalized religious beliefs, attitudes, and feelings become more important with the passing of the years, at least among those to whom they have been important earlier. At the same time it must be emphasized that there may be as high a proportion of unchurched persons among the elderly as in any other population segment. They must be included on the responsibility list of every evangelism committee.[4]

The compelling dynamic of the gospel and the call to justice are powerful motivations for the church to keep elders at the center of its life. These motivations are reinforced strongly by the longtime involvement of older men and women in the church; the meaning they can contribute to and receive from the worship, fellowship, and ministry of a congregation; and the perspective they bring to other persons' understanding and experience of the Christian faith. This is the first focus — on the older adult.

The church also has a highly significant role in relation to the second focus, the focus on all people of whatever years as they are involved in the lifelong aging process (some prefer to call it maturing). The church has a tremendous potential to teach, by precept and example, that life is a continuum — that each successive stage from birth to death has its own significance as part of the whole span. Helping people to age effectively is an aspect of helping them to live effectively. The church is the only institution with the mandate to teach men, women, and children that all through life they belong to God, are created in his image, and are redeemed by his Son.

Yet the church is as guilty as the rest of society of segregating its people according to age. For years it has joined in segregating children and young people in schools and special activities; it also sets elders apart in separate communities and programs. The church has concentrated its systematic educational efforts upon the young, tacitly affirming that human beings stop learning at the end of high school or, perhaps, college. There is also a common tendency among congregations seeking pastors to turn their backs upon candidates in their forties or fifties as too old, and to ask concerning any pastor: "Is he or she able to work with the young people?" There is nothing wrong with being concerned about the church's relationship with the young. Indeed, it can be argued that the young have not been sufficiently involved in the decisions and responsibilities of the life of the church. But when youth are the only group targeted, a congregation may be guilty of a distorted ministry, even from the point of view of young people themselves. A college student showed keen perception when he said: "The youth cult hurts everybody. It robs the young people of a future and makes old age a tragedy. If you reach your peak at 25 and you are over the hill at 30, what do you have to look forward to for the next 40, 50, or 60 years?"[5]

The solution is not to concentrate upon older adults instead of youth, for that would be segregation just as irresponsible as an overemphasis upon youth. What is needed is the clear recognition that human beings of all ages share a common humanity and that all the baptized are fully incorporated into the body of Christ and belong equally to the community of faith. The church in its very nature is multigenerational. It is necessary to manifest these realities of creation and redemption in the church's teaching and program, to demonstrate the meaning and values of each stage of life, and to provide for natural and constructive interchanges among generations.

The basic purpose of this study is to engender constructive attitudes concerning the whole cycle of life, positive rather than negative feelings toward persons who are older, and acknowledgment of the potential of the majority of older women and men for intelligent involvement in the life of church and community.

The very real problems of many of the elderly—in such areas as income maintenance, nutrition, health, housing, transportation, employment and retirement, access to buildings, and educational and cultural activities—must be seriously addressed by the church both in its own programs and in its advocacy on behalf of justice in society. But these problems and the efforts to help solve them must always be seen in terms of the dignity and God-given worth of the human beings involved.

An insidious temptation confronting the church—and every person, group, and institution—is to treat elders paternalistically. To do this is clearly demeaning when caring for invalids confined to nursing-home beds. It is also demeaning when those older persons who are quite capable of living actively are ignored and disparaged simply because they have retired from remunerative employment or have passed a certain age.

Dr. Robert Butler coined the term "ageism," which he defines as "a process of systematic stereotyping of and discrimination against people because they are old, just as racism and sexism accomplish this with skin color and gender. Old people are categorized as senile, rigid in thought and manner, old-fashioned in morality and skills. . . . Ageism allows the younger generations to see older people as different from themselves; thus they subtly cease to identify with their elders as human beings."[6] It is incumbent on the church to combat ageism wherever manifested in its own life, and to acknowledge its elders as members of the community of faith, the universal priesthood of the baptized. Within this context the church's interest should be *both* in what can be done to assist elders who are frail and in need *and also* in how it can keep the door open wide for all older women and men, whatever their circumstances, to participate fully in Christian mission and ministry.

Elders in
Congregational Life

The LCA Social Statement, "Aging and the Older Adult," begins its section on "Congregations" with this paragraph:

> This church should seek older women and men, as it seeks other persons, both as members and as full participants in all dimensions of parish life. Older members are called to share in worship, learning, witness, service and support according to their personal abilities and interests. The congregation is potentially well qualified to engage persons of all ages in activities and relationships which encourage understanding and fellowship across generational lines.

Despite the clear import of these words, it is a rare congregation that takes them seriously. In most parishes that undertake any program at all elders are seen as a special group to be served, cared for, and perhaps entertained, with minimal attention given to helping all people deal with their own aging, see life as a whole, and understand the ministry of the people of God as age-irrelevant.

Service Projects Are Essential — but Not Enough

There are many service projects for older adults that are entirely appropriate for congregational involvement. Examples are visitation of the sick and homebound, telephone reassurance, home repair service, transportation and escort assistance, health services, homemaker programs, "meals on wheels," congregate dinners and fellowship activities, day centers, tours, and financial and other types of counseling. Would that more congregations might initiate these or cooperate with others in them — and do them well.[7]

What Is the Philosophy Behind the Services?

There is, nevertheless, an all-too-prevalent danger. It is the danger of treating older adults as a group of people whom other generously

55

minded members feel moved to help or amuse. The philosophy, the basic attitude, that informs services is extremely important. Are these services rendered with total recognition of the dignity and self-esteem of the elders receiving this ministry, or are they provided, however subconsciously, in a patronizing fashion? Are such services offered in the clear understanding that, with exceptions, they are appropriate only for the minority of elders who are frail or have particular problems? Are older adults given a major responsibility for planning and carrying out services for other older adults? Are such services available to vulnerable persons of other ages as well?

A Reorientation Is Required

These basic questions, however, call for a radical reorientation. If the majority of older men and women are relatively healthy, mentally and spiritually alert, and not nearly as financially burdened as the common myth assumes they are, why should they be brought into parish consciousness primarily as *recipients of service?* If older baptized Christians are full members of the royal priesthood, should they not be full participants in *all* aspects of the ministry of God's people? According to sociologists, most of us tend to behave as we think we are expected to behave. If the church expects older men and women to sit back and rock, regardless of physical or mental condition, in many cases that is what will happen — and the congregation, not to mention the kingdom of God, will be the poorer! But if the church expects elders to employ their talents in significant activities, witnessing, or planning, then, barring ill health or lack of interest, that is what will often happen.

Our Church Is Dying!

A complaint too frequently heard from church members is: "Ours is a dying congregation; with so many older people we have no future." A perception as suicidal as it is common, this can become a self-fulfilling prophecy. The church had better come to grips with this perception because it is based on the theological heresy that the worth of any human being is derived from bases other than the creative and redemptive love of God. The church must also respond to the fact that there are going to be more and more congregations with a majority of older members.

A congregation may indeed be dying, but rarely is it simply because of the age-spread of its members. More often it is because of what the congregation is failing to do. Usually it is failing to meet the needs of both its own people and the immediate community. It is not adjusting its ministry to the changing character of the area it is called by God to serve. In all but a few situations a congregation with a high proportion of older members can carve out a dynamic ministry. When that takes place, then it will likely begin to attract young people, too.[8]

The experience of a congregation in New Mexico[9] clearly demonstrates the validity of this statement. Of the 127 members 74 percent are retired. Almost 57 percent are female. Only 6 percent are under age 23. This is, evidently, an accurate reflection of the composition of the community where the parish is located.

In the mid-1970s the pastor and congregation undertook a project to develop ways in which the priesthood of believers might be realized more completely in the ongoing life of the parish. The concept, set forth in the theme "Ministers — the Entire Church Fellowship," was to become a part of the consciousness of the members "through patterned but normal church activities with strategies to be carefully considered in the context of the historical mission of the church."

A task force established by the Session, the ruling body of the congregation, proposed project objectives and strategies. One Sunday, after a worship service and a covered-dish dinner, the members of the congregation met in small groups to ponder important questions about their life and ministry together, and then met in plenary to gather their ideas, express concerns, and exchange views. Summaries of the small-group conclusions were posted. The Session gave thorough consideration to the reports and approved them.

A group process was the key to developing the goals, objectives, and strategies, and to implementing the strategies. This involved a large number of people and enabled them to see it as their project. One strategy was to organize ways to "help with transportation needs, necessary daily contact, comfort, companionship, positive approaches to attacking loneliness, and readiness to help in any crisis." Another was to encourage better communication among members as family units and/or as individuals. They also decided to initiate a three-week incorporation and assimilation process for new

members designed to help them choose a specific ministry area—
education, service, fellowship, outreach. They further planned to
reclaim inactive members for participation in the ministry of the
parish. Although the list of goals does not include activity in the community, it is stated elsewhere in the report that community involvement has long been a strong tradition in the parish.

The emphases that are most relevant to our present study are:

a. All goals and objectives and all strategies and their implications
   are defined and carried into action through a group process that
   includes a large representation of the membership.

b. A training program is in operation to enable people to function
   in some counseling: in ministry to the ill and the homebound,
   the dying, and the bereaved; and in visitation to prospective
   members, new members, and the inactive. The pastor is
   occupied not only with his own direct ministry but with
   actively equipping the saints for their ministry.

c. All of these acts of ministry are continually stimulated and supported in sermons and teaching situations. Above all, the pastor,
   through public worship, preaching, and the administration of
   the sacraments, regularly interprets what is happening in terms
   of the ministry of the whole people of God.

d. This amazing vitality is displayed in a congregation that
   rejoices in the fact that three-quarters of its members are in
   their older years. There are no pessimistic complaints that "We
   are a dying congregation because so many of our people are
   elders."

Elders Are Part of the Ministry of God's People in the World

Any congregation looks beyond itself to the larger community of
which it is a part. That larger community is not to be seen primarily
as a resource for the enlargement and strengthening of the church.
Rather, the church is called by God to serve his world.

Certainly the church as a corporate body (congregation, synod,
churchwide agency, etc.) ought to serve and witness for justice among
the structures of the secular world—business and industry, government and politics, farms and the press, schools and homes. This
responsibility, however, must not be allowed to hide the fact that the
church is already there in all those spheres of life—in its people. That

is where most of them are, day in and day out. The real task is for the church to *be the church* in and through them — to be, in those places, the church that God intends it to be and claims it to be.

The Christian vocation does not mean to be called to a particular job. We saw in the congregation cited earlier that it is rather to be a member of the church, which the New Testament speaks of as a royal priesthood. In 1 Peter 2:9 (RSV) we read: "But you are a chosen race, a royal priesthood, a holy nation, God's own people, that you may declare the wonderful deeds of him who called you out of darkness into his marvelous light." Christians are to express their vocation, their membership in the priesthood, not only in congregational life but also in the places where they live and work and play, where products are manufactured and decisions are made that affect human lives.

What about elders? The Christian vocation is theirs also. They, too, are part of the royal priesthood. Many older women and men are still employed in the economic and political structures of society. Many more are involved, or have the opportunity to be involved, as volunteers in community service. A host of organizations in every area challenges the potential volunteer to choose carefully where to share talents and time. Government programs, such as Foster Grandparents, the Retired Senior Volunteer Program (RSVP), the Senior Companion Program, and the Service Corps of Retired Executives (SCORE), all open up excellent avenues of service. The National Council on the Aging, aided by many other organizations, is enlisting and training elders to stimulate voter registration not only among older persons but also among the young, the poor and disadvantaged, the unemployed and uneducated, the homebound and disabled — all groups whose registration and voting percentages are low.

A significant way in which elders express their vocation is in their roles of spouse and parent, grandparent and great-grandparent. Many of them can perform some of these roles as surrogates where children or young people do not have actual parents, grandparents, or great-grandparents. There are community and church agencies that structure these kinds of relationships. Such agencies are usually able to give elders information about other opportunities for service.

Older men and women who have reflected seriously on their life-long experience may become unofficial teachers of younger generations. They may be able to help others plumb the depths of experience, and

see life and suffering and death from the perspective of the crucifixion and the resurrection. Some of them will be able and eager to testify to the values of a way of life that is free — free of the domination
of the acquisitive culture so pervasive in the contemporary world.

The congregation should involve elders in its efforts to help people
work through the meaning of the Christian vocation in their lives —
teaching, discussion, support groups. In the process older adults may
arrive at a more distinct understanding of their own roles, their own
calling in the world.

*How Shall the Congregation Respond to
the Characteristics of
"Elders Today and Tomorrow"?*

Policy and programs for the fuller involvement of older adults
should be developed and implemented under the leadership of a
broad-based task force or committee appointed by the church council. This group should include members of various ages (youth, young
adults, the middle-aged, the young-old, and the old-old), both sexes,
whatever racial and ethnic groups are in the parish, and people in
different economic and social circumstances. The task force should
maintain close liaison with all operational committees, and also draw
into its process other parish members, perhaps through small groups,
in developing the recommendations. These recommendations should
then go to the council or the congregation for approval and authori-
zation of further steps.

Along the way the task force ought to gather basic information
about the congregation and the community through a demographic
survey and consultation with knowledgeable community leaders. It
might choose also to review Part One of this study, "Elders Today and
Tomorrow," and ask itself how the characteristics cited relate to
parish programming. Following are several suggestions:

1. Throughout all programs and all the life of the congregation
make certain that elders are regarded and treated as persons, with
their own distinctive histories and relationships and with full membership in the body of Christ.

2. Recognize the validity of the distinction between "young-old"
and "old-old" persons (and other classifications seeking to define
differences between generations in the older years). Be sensitive to the

situations and problems of the young-old, for example, their retirement traumas, losses of varying kinds, decisions that must be made,
the need to use their talents and experiences for the common good,
and the continuing responsibilities some of them carry for the education of children and the care of aged parents. Many of the young-old
should be in important leadership roles in the parish. There is no
justification whatever for retiring them as a group from active participation in church and community.

Be sensitive also to the situation and problems of the old-old (sometimes the young-old, too), for example, decreasing health and
strength, becoming dependent on adult children, and encountering
the losses that tend to multiply with advancing age. The LCA Social
Statement speaks to this dimension of ministry:

> The congregation as a community of faith has unrivaled opportunity
> to assist people, including older men and women, when they experience
> changes in living arrangements, loss of social esteem or physical capac-
> ity, and illness. This is especially true when Christians face the death
> of spouse, other family members or friends, and ultimately their own
> death. Through its ministry of Word and Sacrament, its educational
> ministry, its supportive fellowship and spiritual nurture, the congrega-
> tion can help persons cope with such experiences.

There are many among the old-old who have reasonably good
health and income, who deal constructively with the vicissitudes that
come their way, and who continue to offer effective leadership.
Nevertheless, even in those cases the function of the congregation as
a community of faith can be of the greatest importance.

3. Understand the significance of aging in relation to the worship
of the church. Worship is an act grounded in memory. To worship is
to attribute ultimate worth to God. But behind that is the memory
that God has made us of worth. In the liturgy the community of faith
gathers repeatedly around common symbols that evoke the memory
of the death and resurrection of Jesus Christ, the original event that
called the community into being. If a congregation enters deeply and
fully into the liturgy, then *all* the worshipers, of whatever age, rejoice
not only in the remembrance of what Christ did for us on Calvary
but also in the anticipation of that heavenly banquet which we shall
eat and drink with him in eternal life. In this book, therefore, we do
not speak of developing ways of worshiping that have special rele-

vance for elders. Rather we see that elders have had experiences that should make them responsive to the memory of the past, the intensity of the present, and the hope of the future, all of which are related to the gospel through the liturgy of the church. Older men and women should have something to contribute to the worship of all who belong to the community of faith.[10]

The American Lutheran Church has developed a model by which people in a congregation can allow the liturgy[11] to awaken and deepen their experience of "The Caring Community." A group of thirty-five to seventy persons of all ages commit themselves to meet two hours each week for six to nine months. Sometimes all together, sometimes in smaller, more intimate groups, these women and men and young people follow the sequence of meaning in the Invocation; the Confession, Absolution, and Forgiveness; the Word; the Creed; the Offering; and the Communion. As they open themselves to each other they come to see one another, not as "a mixed group of children, parents, single persons, handicapped, or elderly," but as "persons who know one another." Although "The Caring Community" is still a new approach, those who have been involved testify to changes which occur in their lives, their congregations, their households, and the places where they live and work.[12]

4. Include elders in the evangelism outreach of the congregation and in all efforts to deepen the spiritual life of members. They should be among the workers as well as among those whose response is sought. When members are transferred to other parishes many pastors share with the new congregation information about the needs and skills of the persons or families who are moving. In this process it is important that no exception is made of elders who are transferring. They also have skills and needs that ought to be shared in the new setting.

5. Give special consideration to those elders who have sensory problems, illness or frailty, or who are particularly wedded to familiar ways of doing things (a trait not necessarily peculiar to older people). Frequent changes in liturgical practices, especially without sensitive interpretation, cause difficulty for some older adults — for other persons, too. The concerns of elders regarding hymn choices ought to receive consideration. Particularly for the old-old, the necessity of handling a variety of enclosures or of jumping around from

page to page is too demanding for arthritic hands and failing eyesight. Large-type editions of the service book and other important materials are published and should be made available. It is assumed that nearly all congregations make it possible for sick and shut-in persons who so desire to participate at home in the worship and fellowship of the parish, for example, through regular visits by pastor and lay members, the celebration of the Lord's Supper, and perhaps tape-recordings of the services.

Amplification and hearing-aid devices should be provided in the nave, as well as in rooms used for education and fellowship. If possible hearing aids in the nave should be in different locations rather than concentrated in one area.

The provision of adequate, low-glare lighting, the use of contrasting colors in hallways, rooms, and stairways, and the installation of ramps, railings, nonskid floor coverings, chair lifts, elevators — these and other creative measures will minimize accidents and assist the elderly and persons with handicaps to join in worship, education, and fellowship in the church building.

6. Take cognizance of the situations of nonwhites in congregations and communities in which whites constitute the majority. Are older members of minority groups sought out in the evangelism ministry? Are those who are members of the congregation involved actively in the ministry of the people of God? When they are frail and vulnerable do they receive the same attention from the parish programs of caring? Do they have the same opportunity as others, when necessary, to be admitted to church retirement housing, homes for the aged, and nursing homes?

7. Develop approaches that acknowledge the predominance of women in the older ages, and the fact that large numbers of them are widows. It is essential that parish leaders, and especially a task force on aging, inform themselves about the special problems of older women, for example, their financial situations in relation to Social Security, pensions, and other sources of income, and the fact that widowhood often isolates them from their couple-oriented former associates and the family-centered activities characteristic of the typical congregation. The congregation would do well to institute an AARP Widowed Persons Program[13] or some other program that uses widows and widowers to give support to the newly bereaved. There

should be exploration of ways to come to terms with the prospect that, increasingly, older women will have to associate chiefly with other women. Furthermore, the congregation should challenge older women to use their gifts, training, and experience as responsible leaders and caring workers in the church and in the community, as active participants in the ministry of the church in the world.

8. Discover ways in which a Christian understanding of human sexuality can be effectively conveyed to young and old. This should include efforts to overcome the societal myth that elders have neither the capacity nor the interest for enjoying sexual relations. In its teaching ministry and in its counseling the church should help adult children to be sensitive to the deep need of a widowed or divorced parent for affection not from them alone but, possibly, from a new partner. Finally, the congregation has the obligation to witness to the broader meaning of sexuality — that human beings are sexual beings and that persons of the two sexes may enjoy warm human association without engaging in physical sexual relations. This broader concept can be very important for older women and men.[14]

9. Ponder the following words from the LCA Social Statement, "Aging and the Older Adult." In its section on "Families" the Social Statement declares:

> It is essential to the well-being of all that older men and women be given honor and loving respect, and that in this spirit they be acknowledged as full members of their own families, even if geographically separated, living in an institutional setting, or mentally or physically incapacitated. Every effort must be made to foster wholesome exchange of ideas, sensitive understanding, and mutual communication and helpfulness among generations.

The Social Statement in its section on "Congregations" says:

> The congregation, recognizing that both the positive and negative attitudes of society are found among kinfolk, should strengthen and provide resources to the family as it relates to its older members. It should help the family to cultivate love and respect and a sense of mutual responsibility across the generations, and to be a constructive healing force in all its relationships. The congregation should show equal concern for older persons who are isolated or alienated. Such men and women often have greater needs than do those with a supportive family. It is necessary, therefore, that they be provided with or alerted to alternative supportive relationships, including the congregation's own role as an "extended family."

With these general concepts as a foundation the congregation, perhaps with the aid of a task force and/or a group process, can make specific recommendations concerning families, including the never-married members. It must be open to an understanding of contemporary pressures, particularly those which affect older adults, on families and individuals and also to constructive ways of evaluating changing families in our time. Through all this, however, the reader is reminded that by far the largest number of older men and women are married couples living in their own homes. Extensive surveys have revealed a great deal of happiness among these older households. Although tension and hostility have also been exposed, the proportions of positive and negative atmospheres are not far different from those in younger households.

Let the church work for dynamic families, of whatever form, that involve their members in service to one another, the fellowship of faith, the community and the world.

10. Stay informed about the economic circumstances of elders. While resisting the stereotype that *all* older persons are poor, the congregation must be alert to the serious financial problems that *many* face from day to day. In most parishes there are retirees who have spent their careers specializing in money matters who would be willing to offer financial advice — including guidance with regard to insurance, wills, and deferred giving — to other elders as part of a structured program. Such service should be made available to all, but particularly to elders with lower incomes. Although the program could include tax assistance, it might be better to support and promote the AARP tax help program in the community.[15] The congregation should be prepared to engage in at least three kinds of advocacy. First, it can join other concerned groups in working for legislation that ensures adequate income for older adults.[16] Second, it can become an advocate at various local or regional public offices on behalf of elders who are confused or overwhelmed by bureaucratic procedures. Third, the congregation can use its own channels of interpretation to help destroy the myths about income that underlie the economic plight of too many older adults, for example, the three discussed in Part One: that the poor have only their own improvidence to blame, that jobs are available for elders who want to work, and that Social Security benefits (U.S.) are adequate for the necessities of life.

11. Be sensitive to the multiple medical problems of many elders without succumbing to the stereotype that *all* are ill and in need of care. The fundamental role of the congregation in relation to the health of all its people, including those who are "young-old" and "old-old," is to *be the community of faith*, to be what God intends it to be and empowers it to be.

Special programs and projects should be seen in the context of a fellowship that witnesses to the gospel, stimulates vital interchange among people regardless of age, sex, racial/ethnic heritage, or social/economic status, and challenges all to full involvement (within the limits of health and ability) in the ministry of God's people. This is preventive medicine at its best. It also provides the soundest context for holistic health care, which seeks to deal with every individual who comes for diagnosis and treatment as a whole person with physical, psychological, social, and spiritual needs.

There are parishes that may be large enough to undertake special health programs, such as well-baby clinics, holistic health care centers, and nursing homes. Some programs are entirely appropriate expressions of congregational ministry. Others, however, are open to question. Especially if significant capital expenditure is involved, consideration must be given to the dangers of draining funds from other important needs and of skewing the congregation's ministry to the neglect of other essential tasks. It seems far wiser that, rather than enter into large projects unilaterally, a congregation either join with other congregations (Lutheran or ecumenical) or encourage a community or church agency to take on these responsibilities. It is important and, in many judicatories, required that a congregation considering a major venture of this kind seek the counsel and approval of the leadership of its judicatory. The LCA Division for Mission in North America is working with synods to develop procedures for the guidance of congregations.

Pastors and designated lay persons, including elders, should be well informed about physicians, clinics, hospitals, hospices, and other health services serving their areas, so that they are able to assist elders (and other persons) in need of attention and support. This kind of information should also be provided in the church library. The educational ministry might include periodic sessions on nutrition, exercise, and medical and health matters, with full opportunity for questions and discussion. "Health fairs" or similar programs that provide free (or low-fee) testing and monitoring of the various indicators of the state of health can be sponsored by groups of congregations. These approaches are ingredients of a strategy to foster intelligent and knowledgeable self-help on the part of elders — and others. The congregation should also provide opportunity for examination of the major health and social service delivery systems of society, as well as governmental and "third party" funding systems, to evaluate their performance and accessibility with regard to all people, and make proposals for change.

12. Take seriously the fact that seven out of every ten household heads age 65 and older own their own homes, and that 84 percent of these homes are mortgage-free. Given the significance of home, congregations should devote their efforts to helping elders to remain in their homes *if they wish,* or to move into other living arrangements that permit them to stay independent as long as possible and to continue their association with people and surroundings that have meaning for them. A congregation, synchronizing its work with the community, can use retired carpenters, electricians, and other tradespeople, and skilled young people also, in doing small repair and maintenance jobs on big old houses. It can also obtain or provide supportive homemaker, health, or transportation services that help older adults remain in their own homes or other places of residence in their communities.

Most congregations should not consider sponsoring new housing projects as the primary way to meet the housing needs of elders. Rather, they should explore various options in their communities. What are the quality, cost, and supply of rental housing appropriate to the elderly? Is good public housing available? Are there local community projects, including mobile-home courts, for retirement living? Is it permissible under the law for older people with large homes to create an apartment or apartments in the building? Some church agencies are engaged in matching elders who need accommodations with those who wish to have elders live in their homes. What about group housing where several ambulatory older adults live together in a house with live-in management staff responsible for maintenance, meals, and other necessary care? A number of these under church auspices have appeared in different places. Perhaps a better idea is to have persons of different generations living in such a home. Group housing like this provides many older persons with an option between independent living and institutionalization. Congregations seeking to assist their elders should be acquainted with those residential communities or homes for the aged that are really for housing purposes. The persons who live there are free to come and go and to live independently, but common facilities are on the premises for dining, medical care, fellowship, recreation, and, often, worship. Many such homes are church-related.

When medical needs become too great, it may be necessary for elders to apply to an intermediate care or skilled care home. The move to such a facility is usually a traumatic experience for the older man or woman, the spouse and siblings, and the adult children. The decision should be made responsibly, with the guidance of a skilled counselor, and with an objective evaluation of other alternatives. Insofar as possible, the older person most directly involved should participate in the decision, and, ideally, should visit the home and meet staff and some residents. The congregation should be alert to the emotional problems of the various individuals affected by the drastic change in the elder's life. A significant service can be rendered for family members by support groups dealing with these decisions, guilt feelings, and other problems. Not only the pastor but the congregation as "extended family" has a crucial role. A growing number of Lutheran social mission agencies and institutions are providing seminars and individual counseling for adults facing the problems of aged parents.

For all elders, whatever their circumstances, good housing and good location are necessary to satisfy deep human needs for *independence, security, identity,* and *well-being.*

13. Be cognizant of the increasing educational attainments of older women and men, as pointed up in Part One, "Elders Today and Tomorrow." Education is not the exclusive province of the young; it is for all ages. Congregations, supported by synods and churchwide agencies, face the challenge of providing more substantial educational opportunities for older people as well as persons all along the scale from young to old. The proposals made in Part One are applicable to the church as clearly as to the general community:

a. Education for its own sake. In the congregation there should be more serious educational offerings in theology and biblical studies, ethics and church history, and many other relevant subjects. The congregation should also publicize college level programs for older adults, for example, at Lutheran colleges, other nearby campuses, ELDERHOSTEL, etc.

b. Retirement education. The LCA Division for Parish Services has produced a retirement study program *Ten to Get Ready*,[17] written by Betty and Umhau Wolf. This can be used in any parish. Other excellent books and programs are available.

c. Training of older people for special skills and new fields of service. Congregations need guidance and materials to help them train elders for volunteer activity both in the parish and in the community. Again the Division for Parish Services[18] offers assistance.

d. Education of persons to work with older adults. This is more appropriately a responsibility of social mission agencies or institutions and, perhaps in some cases, of colleges and seminaries. Nevertheless, the intergenerational attitudes and relationships that prevail in the life of a parish will be very influential on the motivation and training of persons who work with elders.

e. Life cycle education. For many years Christian education has stressed the needs and experiences of each separate age-group rather than the common human experience throughout the life span. We are now moving beyond to an affirmation of the family, which is inherently multigenerational, as the primary manifestation of life in its wholeness. Increased research into the older stages of the family life cycle should lead to a more adequate definition of family. People of all ages need to cultivate a fully rounded view of life as a continuum. In Christian education this objective requires an increase in approaches that have already begun to appear, for example, the serious involvement of elders in the education of the young, the sharing of their life stories with people of other ages, the "adoption" of elders by younger families at special seasons, the conscious planning of congregational events that foster face-to-face relationships between generations.[19]

14. Seek creative new ways of increasing opportunities for older men and women to work in employment and/or volunteer activities in the church. Only a few large congregations are able to employ retired pastors or lay persons in various phases of ministry. But all

congregations can improve their recruitment, training, assignment, and retention of volunteers. The Division for Parish Services offers many resources for strengthening the ministry of volunteers in worship and evangelism, education and social ministry, stewardship and financial management. The present study only underscores the importance of determining the talents and experience of older volunteers and involving them in ministries that are necessary, challenging, and appropriate to them. The fact that larger numbers of women, who have often been the chief volunteers, are entering the labor force opens the door for many more elders to become volunteers. As demonstrated by the Presbyterian church in Deming, New Mexico (p. 57), the activity of volunteers has to be placed in the setting of the royal priesthood, the ministry of the holy Christian people. Furthermore, experience makes it clear that the active involvement of the pastor — with organizational support, personal interest, and interpretation from the pulpit — is an essential element in the ministry of volunteers.

15. Take seriously the dramatic increase in the size of the generations age 65 and over, not only in the general population but even more in the membership of most congregations. Take seriously also the changes occurring in elders themselves. Parishes cannot proceed as they have in the past, with some service projects to make the lives of the old folks a little less dull and to comfort them in their declining years. It is to be hoped that the shelving of people who have passed a certain age will soon be out-of-date in parish life. Whether or not younger and middle-aged members see what is happening, "the old folks" increasingly will take hold themselves and assume their share of responsibilities and leadership tasks, especially when the babyboom cohort breaks the situation wide open around the year 2011.

Through all these activities and experiences of congregational life a primary objective should be the intentional cultivation of the spiritual well-being of elders — as well as of all other people. "Spiritual well-being" as a term became prominent in the 1971 White House Conference on Aging, and in subsequent years has been a central concern of the National Interfaith Coalition on Aging (NICA). The word "spiritual" overlaps but is not synonymous with "religious." It is applied also to the appreciation of the beautiful, adjustment to oneself or to others, empathy and sympathy, happiness and sadness, feelings of self-esteem and dignity, the sense of meaning, and many other life experiences and responses. Nevertheless, from the point of view of churches and synagogues, faith in God is an essential dimension of spiritual well-being.

NICA defines spiritual well-being as *"The affirmation of life in a relationship with God, self, community and environment that nurtures and celebrates wholeness."* NICA has developed the following commentary on the definition:

> The *spiritual* is not one dimension among many in life; rather, it permeates and gives meaning to all life. The term spiritual well-being, therefore, indicates wholeness in contrast to fragmentation and isolation. "Spiritual" connotes our dependence on the source of life, God the creator.
>
> What, then, is spiritual well-being? We cannot regard well-being as equated solely with physical, psychological, or social good health. Rather, it is an *affirmation of life*. It is to say "yes" to life in spite of negative circumstances. This is not mere optimism which denies some of life's realities; rather, it is the acknowledgment of the destiny of life. In the light of that destiny it is the love of one's own life and of the lives of others, together with concern for one's community, society, and the whole of creation, which is the dynamic of spiritual well-being.
>
> A person's affirmation of life is rooted in participating in a community of faith. In such a community one grows to accept the past, to be aware and alive in the present and to live in hope of fulfillment. Affirmation of life occurs within the context of one's relationship with God, self, community, and environment. God is seen as Supreme Being, creator of life, the source and power that wills well-being. All people are called upon to respond to God in love and obedience. Realizing we are God's children, we grow toward wholeness as individuals, and we are led to affirm our kinship with others in the community of faith as well as the entire human family. Under God and as members of the community of faith, we are responsible for relating the resources of the environment to the well-being of all humanity.
>
> Human wholeness is never fully attained. Throughout life it is a possibility in process of becoming. In the Judeo-Christian tradition(s) life derives its significance through its relationship with God. This relationship awakens and nourishes the process of growth toward wholeness in self, crowns moments of life with meaning, and extols the spiritual fulfillment and unity of the person.[20]

Since these words grew out of interfaith reflection, each faith group must translate their essential content into terms appropriate to its own perspective. Spiritual well-being gives a person—of whatever age—the unity of purpose and inner strength to live life in such a way that physical and economic factors are no longer decisive, that human relationships have greater depth, and that the losses of the years and the certainty of death are met in faith and hope. There is nothing more crucial for a congregation to do than to cultivate spiritual well-being in elders. This objective, intentionally and creatively pursued, must pervade everything the congregation does with regard to aging and the older adult.

From the Lutheran perspective, the whole life of the church has its unique basis in the Word and the sacraments. The Augsburg Confession, Article VII, declares: "The church is the assembly of saints in which the Gospel is taught purely and the sacraments are administered rightly."[21] God's unconditional love is mediated through worship and preaching, counseling and pastoral care, evangelism and social ministry, through the total witness of God's people in God's world. In this all-encompassing ministry there are no dividing lines according to age!

Elders and the Church's Agencies and Institutions

The Lutheran Church in America, through its synods, relates to a network of 130 health and welfare agencies and institutions. They are responsible for a wide range of services to people of all ages and in all sorts of circumstance—health ministries, mental health, acute care, long-term care, rehabilitation, hospice, chemical dependency, social services, family services, ministry to seafarers, refugee/immigrant services, assistance to congregations. Some of these ministries are provided through statewide multiservice agencies, others through individual nursing homes or service programs reaching a specialized or a relatively local constituency. Some services are rendered by professionally trained staff; others are not. Some agencies or institutions are integral parts of the work of a synod; others are more loosely related. Some belong only to the LCA; others belong to two or three church bodies. In a large number of cases older adults are the chief recipients of service or care.[22]

The LCA Social Statement Provides
a Basis for Policy

In 1968 the LCA in convention adopted the Social Statement, "The Church and Social Welfare." The following affirmations from that statement are a sound basis for policy:

a. This church reaffirms its belief that social welfare services carried on through the church either in its individual or corporate expression are a joyous and selfless response of love growing out of faith in Christ.
b. This church in order to fulfill its service role should carry on continual study, research and experimentation in the field of social welfare.
c. This church should be flexible in its social policies and prac-

73

tices. The diversity and complexity of modern society are such that a variety of responses to any problem may be appropriate.

d. This church should be alert to the manner in which social need is met, whether by government, voluntary, church, or proprietary agency. Wherever practice or policy threatens the rights and dignity of those who require aid, the church should strive to bring about correction.

e. This church's concern may be expressed by the development of agencies and institutions when community need calls for them. They are not to be ends in themselves, but are to be seen as part of the total engagement of the church.

f. When this church establishes social welfare programs it may properly enter into agreements with federal, state and local government to receive payment for services rendered or to accept, on a nonpreferential basis, grants or long-term loans.

g. This church through its various jurisdictions should support social welfare services by providing opportunity for financial participation by its congregations and their individual members through both general benevolence and direct personal giving, in keeping with the established policies of the appropriate synod(s).

h. The social welfare services of this church should comply with the service standards set by government, professional agencies and the church.

i. This church should serve all people in its related social service programs.

j. This church in its social welfare activities should, so far as it is possible, involve those for whom service is intended in determining the services and the manner in which they are administered.[23]

It is clear that the LCA sees its agencies and institutions of health and social service as important parts of its ministry to the contemporary world. In keeping with that important role the church expects them to meet the highest standards of health, safety, and service, and to view themselves in light of the servant ministry of the people of God. They have an essential place in this study. In response to the demographic and other information presented in Part One, "Elders Today and Tomorrow," the following suggestions are made for consideration in the church's health and social service planning.

Suggestions for Response to
"Elders Today and Tomorrow"

1. Take seriously the revelation that every older woman and man is a person created in God's image and redeemed by the blood of Jesus Christ. Since agencies and institutions deal primarily with the most vulnerable of elders, they face the strongest temptation to view them en masse or to categorize them according to sex or racial/ethnic group, the nature of illness or degree of disability, or even their financial status in relation to the cost of care. Those who spend their time working with the frail aged are also in the greatest danger of projecting the afflictions and characteristics of the people they serve onto the large majority of elders — most of whom do not share these afflictions and characteristics. Thus it may happen that the persons most dedicated in service and most knowledgeable about aging help perpetuate negative stereotypes of older adults.

2. Take cognizance of the fact that one of every three young-old persons (c. 55–75 years of age) has one or both parents living. This means that at the very moment when these persons are facing their own retirement experience and possibly are still repaying loans for their children's education, they now carry the psychological and financial burden of caring for fathers and/or mothers who may be ill or incapacitated. Futhermore, it is often true that when public funds like those from Medicaid are used for the support of an older man or woman in nursing care nothing is available to sustain the spouse who remains at home.

Since many of the persons involved in these difficult situations are within range of the ministry of LCA-related agencies and institutions, these organizations have a unique opportunity to struggle with such problems and devise ways — regular seminars, counseling services, etc. — to help spouses, adult children, and other family members in working them through. Many now have programs to assist in these situations.

3. Remove the barriers that prevent service to and employment of older people from all racial/ethnic groups who live in the constituency area.

4. Sponsor agency programs to help women and men deal with bereavement and with the trauma of being a widow or a widower. This should include skilled counseling, arrangements whereby indi-

vidual widowed persons help those newly experiencing bereavement, and group sessions in which recently bereaved men and women meet regularly to assist one another. The Widowed Persons Program of AARP is one of a number of examples of effective efforts.

Agencies can be of help to nearby congregations by providing competent leadership for programs of this type or by offering consultation to help congregations develop their own.

5. Arrange sex education programs that give adequate attention to the sexuality of older adults. This is essential for the general public, for elders themselves, and for those who work with them. Somehow the demeaning myths concerning the sexuality of elders must be destroyed, and an effective agency should be able to make a good contribution to the objective. A well-planned educational program can do battle with the myth that older men and women do not and ought not to have interest in sex, with the reluctance of many adult children to encourage a widowed parent in remarriage, and with the failure of many nursing homes to affirm the sexuality of residents in their living arrangements and provisions for privacy. Although the physical expressions of sexuality are important for most people, even in the older years sexuality must be recognized as a basic factor in human relationships far beyond the physical.

6. Examine carefully the family, particularly in relation to older women and men. What are families like in the area served by the agency, both inside and outside the churches? What changes are taking place and how are these changes actually affecting elders? How can the agency support older families, the majority of which are likely to consist of husband-wife households living in their own homes? How can the agency emphasize the meaning of the family for elders — a vehicle for social and psychological continuity, personal interaction, and support through affection? Many agencies are dealing with these questions through counseling and group techniques.

Agencies also have a challenge to help people with the problems that come from divorce, which involve more persons than the separating partners and their children. Grandparents and great-grandparents are affected in their relationships with new daughters-in-law and sons-in-law, and their grandchildren and stepgrandchildren. Unmarried or widowed aunts and uncles are also affected. More research is needed into the confusion that may grow out of these marital changes. Still another area in which agencies may make a distinct contribution is the effect on elders of the increasing employment of women outside the home, and the effect upon these women when they become elders.

Many agencies can play some role in dealing with the problems of family violence, as described in "Elders Today and Tomorrow." The role may involve education, counseling, or actual intervention. Intervention, of course, calls for special training and skills, usually involving an interagency, multiprofessional response. LCA agencies can prepare themselves to provide direct service, cooperate with public resources, help pastors to develop skills and insights, and assist congregations to become supportive communities.

It is recognized that agencies and institutions vary widely in their ability to deal with issues of this sort. Nevertheless, even those whose functions do not include education or community action must study seriously how the elders they seek to serve are affected by what happens in families, and must allow their programs to be influenced by the insights they gain.

It is a worthy objective for this church and its agencies and institutions to foster a dynamic view of the family within which all members, including elders, can find strength amid the changes that all must face.

7. Consider providing competent financial education and counseling, available to the public directly through agency programs or indirectly through congregations. Education and counseling might cover subjects such as the significance of adequate income for elders; the facts of the current economic situation; information on Social Security, Medicare/Medicaid, Supplementary Security Income (SSI), food stamps, pension systems, and comparable programs in Canada; and the deeper financial predicament of minority-group persons, women, single elders, and the oldest individuals and families.

Perhaps one of the most important topics for candid discussion is the popular attitude toward poverty among the elderly, the essentially tragic tendency of our society to ease men and women out of employment at an arbitrary age (regardless of what the law may say), and then to depreciate them as "unproductive." This negative attitude expresses itself sometimes in the way government leaders talk about income programs for the elderly. A recent cartoon shows an older couple going to the rural mailbox in front of their shack. The wife describes one item: "It's our monthly payment from Social Security, with a little note saying there's no need to worry, the government has worked out a funding solution for the program, but strongly implying that it would be a big help if we dropped dead a little earlier than usual."[24] Are there effective ways in which an agency can contribute to more constructive thinking about older adults and income programs?

8. Move into the vanguard of creative thinking and action with regard to health care. The health and social service agencies and institutions of the church touch the lives of thousands of older women and men, especially in the area of health care. They have more freedom to act than do the public institutions and programs governed at every step by laws and regulations. What a fine opportunity many of the church's agencies and institutions have to influence the direction that health care will take in the future. Our hospitals, in particular, can exert this influence from within "the system." The following emphases are worthy of consideration:

a. The reorientation and restructuring of the medical profession and the health system so that they can deal more adequately with whole persons. This calls for renewed concentration upon preventive medicine, self-help, and the training of physicians to recognize and respond to the social, economic, and psychological factors that are vital ingredients in physical and mental illness. Although it has become a cliché to say that the United States has a "sickness care" system rather than a "health care" system, there is enough truth in the cliché to justify its being heard.

Vast sums of money are poured into the treatment of specific diseases or conditions as compared with the paltry sums expended to help people take care of themselves through sound nutrition, good exercise, regular dental care, a healthful environment, and a wholesome philosophy of life.

b. The need for research and medical care to give as much attention to the chronic diseases of old age as has been given to the acute diseases more common to youth and middle age. Since more persons are now in long-term care institutions on any given day than are in hospitals, it is imperative that physicians be better prepared to deal with older people. Responsibility, of course, goes back to the 126 medical schools that ought to train students in geriatrics. Some but not necessarily all of these schools should have departments of geriatrics as bases for research and specialization. The others should seek to incorporate an understanding of the special requirements of older people in specialties such as urology, orthopedics, and gynecology. Courses and lectures imparting geriatric knowledge should be required, since only 2 percent of medical students choose electives in this field. These same students, in the prime of their careers, will probably be devoting 50 percent of their time to older adults. This more well-rounded medical education, some of which might take place in the church's institutions, will help wipe out the stereotypes that many doctors hold about the illnesses of elders; they will not be as ready to incorrectly diagnose a treatable disease by calling it normal aging.

c. The need to rectify the bias of the health system in the direction of the institutional care of older people. Strongly encouraged by the same bias in Medicare and Medicaid, even the church has tended to be overcommitted toward moving elders too quickly into long-term care situations, sometimes inappropriately. For years forward-looking leaders have advocated a far more extensive development of home health care, along with other kinds of supportive services, many of them nonmedical, that can assist older persons to remain in their own homes or other places of residence.[25] Why have these tested and proven approaches not caught on as they should? Why do people, both within the church and in the general community, move so readily into the erection of expensive institutions, paying little attention to noninstitutional programs?

A number of the health and social service agencies and institutions of the LCA are becoming trailblazers, influencing the whole health system "from within" to change its approaches and advocating radical new changes in Medicare and Medicaid to undergird these new approaches.

To be sure, the enormous growth of the older population

makes necessary the continued building of nursing homes. Agencies of the church, however, are broadening their approach. They are intensifying their efforts to sponsor "communities" that offer a continuum of care, with single complexes providing a range from independent living to intermediate care to skilled nursing care. And many of the same agencies are broadening their approach even more, as they lay greater stress upon ministries in the larger community and encourage independent living for elders to the fullest extent possible. The church should support these trends.

   d. A strategy to deal with the health problems of chemical misuse, abuse, and dependency among elders. More than a million elders in the United States are problem drinkers, and large numbers have difficulties with the misuse of prescription and over-the-counter drugs, as described in "Elders Today and Tomorrow." Health and social service agencies and institutions have the responsibility, when it is appropriate to their designated functions, to offer programs that can help individuals directly and also assist congregations in helping them. They also have responsibility to be well acquainted with qualified drug and alcohol treatment centers to which they can make referrals. The church's agencies and institutions can make a significant contribution to the reduction of the number of wasted lives, family turmoil, serious illness, and unnecessary death.

  9. Explore ways to help older men and women with their housing problems. It is in harmony with the purpose of many agencies and institutions to provide home repair and maintenance services to older people living in large, older homes that are becoming more difficult to keep in good condition. It is also appropriate to offer transportation and escort assistance, or to guide congregations in offering these services. An agency's counseling program might also help older persons decide how to renovate present housing or how to secure new housing if that is desirable. Possibly the agency will wish to start and supervise a share-a-home type of program, in which a carefully matched younger person moves into an older person's home,[26] or a group of ambulatory elders live together in a house with live-in assistance for maintenance and other services. The agency should be ready

to press government to provide good public housing at reasonable cost, and may choose to initiate or join in the development of retirement housing suitable for elders with different incomes. In any case, every effort must be made to preserve the atmosphere and values of home for older women and men.

It is assumed that an agency or institution working with the elderly will be sensitive to the plight of aged parents who have been separated from children and grandchildren by the moving of the younger family(ies). It should be recognized that geographical distance does not break already warm relationships (modern communications and rapid transportation help hold families together, in the case of people able to afford these), nor does close proximity ensure affection. This may be especially true in some situations where elderly parents live with adult children. An agency or institution serving elders needs to be keenly aware of the dynamics that may be at work in these and other circumstances and use all the skills available in its professional personnel to resolve tensions and improve human relationships. It should also plan seminars to help pastors and congregations include this dimension in their ministries.

Wherever an agency or institution of health or social service is located — urban, suburban, town, or country — it should stay up-to-date on what is happening to older people in its area, and project programs that are relevant. In all situations it is essential to cooperate with public agencies and community organizations and ecumenical bodies in as united an approach as possible.

10. Join hands with congregations and with other community and governmental agencies to assist persons who have been returned to their communities because of the recent trend toward deinstitutionalization. Many who have been released from state mental hospitals in these well-intentioned programs are elders. The problem is that support services in the communities have not been prepared to accept and assist these people. Many have fallen prey to ill-managed boarding homes; others wander the streets or live miserably in abandoned buildings. These persons are greatly in need of the ministry of the church and its agencies.

11. Respond to the needs of adults released from the criminal justice system. The number of such persons who are age 60 or over is much higher than we are likely to expect. Their need for community

orientation and support is very great. This also challenges both congregations and social mission agencies who are concerned about the plight of human beings.

12. Be alert to the increasing educational attainments of older women and men, and the changes that are likely to take place in their abilities, attitudes, and demands. Agencies might ask themselves which of the new educational needs they are able to help meet.[27] At the minimum most agencies, it would seem, must provide or avail themselves of programs educating persons, whether paid employees or volunteers, who will work with older adults. Along with specific training for particular jobs, the scope of such education should include not only the characteristics and ailments of the frail elderly with whom most of these persons will work but also the characteristics and potentials of the large number of older adults who will not be under their care. Indeed, elders certainly should be among the care givers who receive the training and participate actively in the work. Pastors also should be given special attention in this kind of continuing education, so that they may relate more effectively to their older members, stimulate dynamic parish programs that involve all people regardless of age or other temporal distinctions, and interpret the significance of the whole span of human life.

Many agencies may also sponsor programs of retirement education or assist parishes in doing so. And many may choose to provide training for elders in special skills for new careers or new volunteer activities.

13. Consider employing older men and women in the work of the agency or institution. This should include, when appropriate, important responsibilities that make use of talents and experience accumulated through the years. The challenges posed by M. H. Beach, as quoted on pages 40–41, may be addressed also to the church and its agencies and institutions.

Elders also have immense potential for volunteer work in agencies and institutions. Volunteers must be recruited and trained as creatively and thoroughly as paid workers, and they must be assigned, perhaps for specified terms, to positions appropriate to what they have to offer. Wise supervision of the program is just as important as wise supervision of professional and support personnel.

There must be special concern that volunteers not be used simply to avoid paying for the work. A woman wrote recently: "One thing I find is that there is a lot of volunteer work offered elderly people. In my way of thinking this is slave labor. They tell us this will make us feel good. Well, what I need is grocery money." Let not the church's agencies and institutions be guilty of exploitation of elders or anyone else!

14. Make use of the political clout of elders themselves in making contact with government officials in the interest of policies and laws that advance justice and human fulfillment. They should be used — if they desire — in both the decision-making and action phases of advocacy. Agencies should recognize that the concerns of older adults are not confined to the effects of public policies on themselves and their peers. They are and will be deeply interested in issues of peace and war, the rights of women and minority-group persons, the environment, and the political leadership of their nations. We must not stereotype the most diverse segment of the population, and of the church's membership, as the "aging vote."

15. Take seriously and rejoice in the prospect that elders will become more assertive as the years move on. Care givers are tempted, often subconsciously, to see themselves in the position of "caring" and "serving," and the adults with whom they work as "patients" or "clients," rather than as persons of dignity and individuality. The elders of the future, at least large numbers of them, will not stand still for this attitude. Inside the institutions, they will want to have important roles in policy making and the monitoring of administration and care giving. They may ask for representation on boards and in management. Out in the community they may be much more aggressive than is the case today in fostering home health care and other supportive services that enable even vulnerable elders to care for themselves in their own homes or their home neighborhoods. Older persons will surely support the maintenance of intermediate and skilled care nursing homes, which will be even more badly needed than now, but they may not support them as automatically and uncritically as do many elders of the present.

16. Be alert to both the responsibility and the opportunity offered by the increasing mobility of some older adults. First, the fact of mobility underscores the importance of more intentional cross-fertilization of program planning and strategies among Lutheran

social mission agencies and institutions across the land, in the interest of the greater health and well-being of the elders they serve. Second, in view of the growing practice of relatively affluent older members of congregations to live part of each year in the South and part in the North, agencies and institutions might consult with each other about how the skills and needs of these persons can be systematically communicated. The advantage of such a system would be evident not only in better service to elders in their needs but also in the sharing of talent.

Elders and the Church's Programs of Education

Theological Schools

One of the crucial tasks of the church is the education of its professional leadership, primarily its pastors. As servants of the Word, pastors are the teachers of teachers and inevitably initiators of most of the things that happen in the church. Through preaching, witnessing, counseling, and administrative work they touch thousands of lives and share a mutuality of ministry with the laity. The role of a theological seminary is to give pastors and other leaders the intellectual tools, the spiritual insights, and the practical skills to perform competently the tasks committed to them.

It seems obvious that exposure to the aging process and the concerns of older adults should be part of the education of pastors and other professional leaders. It is a safe guess that a very large percentage of the members of most congregations are elders, and that half of the average pastor's work is with older women and men. This can only increase steadily as the demographic revolution intensifies. How are pastors and other leaders to grow in their ministry to and with this important segment of the population unless a basic understanding of aging and the older adult is part of their educational preparation? Furthermore, all people, regardless of their years, are going through the lifelong aging process. Pastors and other leaders need assistance in order to help the young and middle-aged deal with their aging.

Yet the subject of gerontology (study of aging) is only beginning to appear in current theological curricula. A computer check of the literature concerning theological education reveals very little material that seeks to relate aging issues to the theology of the church. Gerontology, moreover, has not been among the priorities for planning in theological education. In 1975 the Association of Theological Schools sponsored a Project on Readiness for Ministry. This comprehensive project established criteria which were considered important for the ordained ministry. Among the 444 criterion statements one reads this way: "Works to improve community service to older persons." This item, which occurs also in another place, is the only direct reference to aging in the entire report. In contrast, youth are referred to on at least 13 pages of the 140-page document, and ten items explicitly mention youth. One-third of the 64 criterion clusters consists of topics pertinent to the pastor's relating well to children and youth. Sensitivity to aging, clearly, is not perceived as a priority, at least it was not in 1975, for the training of a pastor or the assessment of his or her ministry.[28]

The Seminary Has a Leadership Role in Theological Reflection on Aging

A theological school is in a unique position to stimulate theological reflection upon aging. A large number of the increasing throng of men and women who are living into the older years are healthier, better educated, and have higher incomes than their parents or grandparents. How shall they be used as a valuable human resource in the parish and the community? Many elders have serious problems of health, finances, housing, self-esteem. How shall they be enabled to deal with such problems in ways that support their dignity and individuality? How shall all persons be assisted to discover what the Christian vocation means for them at every stage of life — including the later years?

These are down-to-earth issues that every pastor, every professional leader, every member of the people of God must face as a part of living. The LCA Social Statement, "Aging and the Older Adult," declares: "God's love for all persons is creative and unconditional. Human beings have dignity not because they have achieved success or the esteem of the world, but because they are made in the image of God. They are given the capacity to relate to God in responsible freedom." The schools of theology are places where faculty and students can reflect upon the implications of God's creative and unconditional love for all persons and internalize this understanding as they look at their own aging and relate to those who are older.

Pastors, like many other people, are victims of negative stereotypes of elders and the aging process. Too often they see most older persons more as recipients of services than as participants in the church's mission, and assume that a congregation with a large number of older men and women is dying. Pastors themselves frequently join in segregating people according to age and fail to acknowledge the richness of the whole span of life from birth to death. They are not immune to the "work ethic" syndrome which suggests that a human being's value is derived from his or her productivity. Gerontophobia, the fear of age, hampers the relationships of many pastors with older adults. These are all concerns that have psychological and sociological dimensions, but they also involve theological issues of legitimate interest to the seminaries.

The church and its people need theological understanding of the relation of faith to loss, bereavement, suffering, and dying, and, through it all, to the deeply joyous celebration of grace. Certainly the school of theology has a teaching role in this. The ways in which these and other theological issues relevant to aging and the older adult are resolved will influence the self-understanding and pastoral attitudes of ministers and other professional leaders and also the directions of ministry in the church's congregations.

A theological seminary may have gerontology courses in its curriculum, taught either by faculty members who have secured special training in that field or by competent teachers from other educational institutions. Or the seminary may arrange for its students to take courses at university institutes of gerontology. Whatever the approach, if it is not feasible to require this work, efforts should be made to persuade students of its importance to their pastoral ministry.

Theological schools have an acknowledged problem in introducing the subject of aging into their curricula. Through the years they have been bombarded with requests to give special attention to "causes" that have arisen out of the experience of the church, for example, evangelism, stewardship, economic justice, chemical dependency, world mission, ecumenism. It has been difficult for seminaries to include them because of the need to integrate basic biblical, historical-theological, and functional subjects into three short years of course work.

Nevertheless, there are Lutheran theological schools where the dimension of aging is being effectively included. Melvin A. Kimble, professor of Pastoral Theology and Ministry at Luther Northwestern Theological Seminary, St. Paul, Minnesota, is introducing a concentration on gerontology with a sequence of courses in the middle and senior years that will provide up to thirty hours of education, including intentional internship and clinical experiences.

In the late 1970s the National Interfaith Coalition on Aging, enabled by a grant from the U.S. Administration on Aging, conducted Project GIST (Gerontology in Seminary Training). Project GIST gathered sixty participants[29] from many religious bodies, most of them from seminary faculties, to explore the possibilities for teaching gerontology in schools of theology. Each participant designed and implemented an eighteen-month educational project intended to make an impact upon the seminary curriculum and/or continuing education programs for use with clergy and lay leaders.

A major product of Project GIST is the document, "Education for Ministry in Aging: Guidelines for Competency Objectives."[30] Jesse H. Ziegler, former executive director of the Association of Theological Schools, suggests the use of the guidelines "as a part of a total description of desired educational outcomes, leaving it to each seminary faculty to do its own hard work of curriculum design and deployment of educational resources to accomplish those outcomes. To that process the guidelines clearly give an interested faculty a 'great step up'."[31]

In addition to having gerontology courses in the seminary curriculum, there are ways of teaching the issues of aging in the midst of many disciplines. In some LCA seminaries aging is being introduced into various courses. For example, at Luther Northwestern Seminary an older person is invited to participate in an Old Testament course on suffering. In a New Testament course students are given assignments to write Bible studies for the frail elderly and to prepare courses for retired persons and for residents of nursing homes. At the Lutheran Theological Seminary at Gettysburg, Pennsylvania, Professor J. Russell Hale deals with aging in his church and society courses and in the seminary extension program. It is to be hoped that systematic theologians will see aging as a dimension of life that is worthy of their most careful thought and writing.

This approach of teaching gerontology in the midst of various disciplines does not require that all theological professors be experts in that field. It does suggest, however, that all might have enough generalist knowledge to see how the issues of aging intersect with their disciplines and may be enlightened by them. Since learning is accomplished through informal as well as formal methods, faculty members should be well enough informed and sensitized to be free of myths and fallacies about aging, and able to articulate positive understandings.

The Seminary Has a Role as a Community

Since a theological school is both a learning and a ministering community, it is desirable that men and women of various ages be members of that community. This is happening today with the presence of both female and male students and of families on the campus. The age-spread is being augmented by the influx of many older students into school, and by the contributions made to the community by retired professors and other older scholars. Beyond this many elders would like to attend seminary courses for personal enrichment and for the enhancement of their participation in church and society. Others would be happy to assist as resource persons in classes where their memories and experience might add perspective. Intergenerational sharing provides fruitful opportunities for young and old to reflect together on how biblical and theological sources speak to relationships that are intrinsic to life.

Internship Offers Experience with Aging and the Older Adult

If the seminary helps sensitize students to the problems and potentials of growing older, those students as they become interns in congregations will be able to observe and listen intelligently to older adults and to raise questions about the role of elders in parish life. As part of their internship many students might be placed deliberately in situations that provide association with older women and men, both those who are frail and/or institutionalized and those who are healthy and vigorous. These experiences, of course, will be made more valuable by in-depth reflection on them with theological professors, other students, older persons at the seminary, and gerontology specialists.

Continuing Education Reaches Pastors and
Other Professional Leaders

Theological schools conduct various kinds of continuing education programs, sometimes on campus but also in other communities. They may be in the form of occasional seminars or convocations, or they may consist of regular graduate school sessions held weekly. Continuing education provides an excellent opportunity to lead pastors and other professional leaders, whether active or retired, to an understanding of the lifelong aging process, needs and resources of elders, and program possibilities in the congregation and the community. It is hoped that seminaries will continue gerontology as a staple of their continuing education curricula.

As the church responds to vast demographic changes, the current and future characteristics of elders, and its theological imperatives, the seminaries have a place in the front line. They are the teachers of the church's pastors and other professional leaders and have great influence and responsibility in defining and interpreting the faith.

Colleges and Universities

Through its synods the Lutheran Church in America relates to twenty-two colleges and universities in the United States and Canada. Although many tend to think of these institutions as serving only the young, there are persuasive arguments for seriously including middle-aged and older adults as beneficiaries of higher education. Indeed a number of the LCA colleges and universities are taking some initial steps in that direction. The action suggestions that follow are intended both to affirm what is being done and to challenge the colleges and universities to devise further strategies for involving older adults more fully in classroom and campus life.

Many Elders Welcome College-Level
Educational Opportunities

Church-related colleges and universities have much to offer older women and men with regard to education for its own sake—education for life enrichment. Rabbi Abraham Heschel delivered a now-famous address, "To Grow in Wisdom," to the 1961 White House Conference on Aging. Calling old age "a major challenge to the inner life," he proposed that a home for the elderly have not only a director of recreation but also "a director of learning in charge of intellectual activities." Furthermore, Rabbi Heschel said: "What the nation needs is senior universities, universities for the advanced in years where wise men should teach the potentially wise, where the purpose of learning is not a career, but where the purpose of learning is learning itself."

The interest of older people in college level education is clearly demonstrated by the ELDERHOSTEL phenomenon. Founded in 1975 by Martin P. Knowlton and David Bianco, ELDERHOSTEL is a program whereby educational institutions offer weeklong selections of challenging courses taught by members of their own faculties. Older men and women — hostelers — live in student accommodations, take courses, and have access to libraries and campus facilities at a weekly tuition charge ($180 at the time of this writing). Marty Knowlton had the passionate conviction that:

> Older adults would benefit even more from a liberal arts education than traditionally younger students. Adults, for one thing, knew how to ask questions. They were not passive or naive, either. With a lifetime of experience, older adults could grasp the meaning of a subject more quickly than a youngster, and they could easily form ideas and opinions of their own. Furthermore, people who had already had careers, raised families and had tasted life could appreciate education for itself, rather than for its more practical value in improving one's career prospects. To be enlightened, to increase one's sense of accomplishment and self worth through learning — these were the things that they sought.[32]

Knowlton's prophetic vision has been vindicated — dramatically. In the summer of 1975, five New Hampshire institutions opened their doors to two hundred eager pioneer Elderhostelers. Since then the network has grown to seven hundred institutions hosting seventy thousand hostelers, with the program coordinated by a Boston-based headquarters.

A number of LCA colleges and universities are part of the ELDERHOSTEL network. Other schools, though not involved in ELDERHOSTEL, welcome older adults to audit regular courses or take them for credit, sometimes free of charge or with reduced tuition. Some LCA colleges offer special educational programs for older persons. Their motivations are the same as those that established

ELDERHOSTEL. An additional incentive is that the presence of elders in the classroom with younger students can vitalize the educational environment, lengthen perspectives, and broaden and deepen learning experiences. The enrollment of more elders will help the institutions compensate, though probably not fully, for the declining enrollment of the young during the immediate future. Nevertheless, the primary reasons for colleges to reach out toward older adults lie deeper than self-preservation.

Can Educational Financial Aid Be Provided for Elders?

Educational institutions and governmental bodies should consider the appropriateness of financial aid to older adults, many of whom live on radically reduced incomes following retirement. Harold L. Hodgkinson raises the issue:

> The normal arguments for investing in human resource development (access to the world of work, increasing productivity, etc.) do not apply, yet the person's educational needs may be very real and important. We also know that our elderly population will continue to improve in general health and vitality and will want to play a significant role in American life. Their numbers will be formidable in a political sense, and they vote in very large numbers. Education may well become one of the major issues on their agenda in the next two decades.[33]

The same issue is applicable to federal and state aid and also to financial assistance to older students provided by the institutions themselves.

All Students Need to Understand Lifelong Aging

Colleges or universities should explore ways to bring the concept of the full life cycle into the education of students of all ages. The myths and stereotypes of aging, just as evident on the campus as anywhere else, reflect not only misinformation and insensitivity but also deep fears of aging and of death. The result is that younger and middle-aged persons become adept at holding older men and women at arm's length, a negative stance that is facilitated by imagining *all* elders to be physically ill or weak, mentally confused, and socially in retreat.

One way in which an educational institution can approach this challenge is to include gerontology courses in its curriculum and also to include a gerontological dimension in various disciplines, for example, social gerontology in the sociology department, the psychology of aging in the psychology department, the political consequences of aging in political science. Colleges and universities will do well to seek the assistance of academic institutes of gerontology in training professors, securing guest lecturers, and building this program.

A second way to approach the challenge is to sponsor continuing education courses, seminars, and intergenerational activities regarding aging and the older adult that involve faculty and students, alumni and the general public.

A third way is to encourage the participation of faculty and students in church and community programs working with elders. Gettysburg College has a community service program that engages one hundred students in visitation at local homes and institutions for the aged, as well as field trips that expose students to gerontological concerns.

A fourth way, perhaps the most basic of all, is to provide opportunities for students and faculty to mingle naturally with alert and active elders who take regular courses, live in residence halls, and participate in other areas of campus life. Some educational institutions recruit older men and women as volunteer resource persons who share their recollections and insights in classes in history, sociology, or literature. California Lutheran College has a lifelong learning program that includes a Senior Fellows component. Retired persons are invited to be residents on campus for specified terms. They share in college life and provide services in their particular areas of expertise, whether academic, administrative, or technical.[34]

A significant contribution to intergenerational experiences can be made by older scholars and emeritus professors who continue to use the library, give lectures, and attend campus events. Furthermore, some colleges, again including California Lutheran, make a practice of securing the services of professors who have retired from other faculties. Since on this basis some schools are able to obtain persons of greater ability and reputation than might otherwise be possible, this arrangement will often benefit the institution academically beyond whatever benefit may come to the retired professors. Nevertheless, these visiting teachers along with those retired from the college itself and the older members of the active faculty are living examples that the life of the mind does not go into decline after age 35.

Elders Are Changing in Educational Status

Colleges and universities related to the church should be prepared to respond creatively to the increasing educational attainments of older women and men. Earlier in this study it was stated that when the "baby-boom" people become 65 years of age and above, 90 percent of them will be high-school graduates and 27 percent of the men and 20 percent of the women will be college graduates. Will the LCA colleges and universities be prepared to deal with the educational interests of this kind of older population? Will they help to provide education for its own sake? Will they help older people to retool for further careers?

Educational leaders, however, dare not merely look ahead to an exciting future. There are stark realities to be faced today. About one-seventh of the current older population in the United States are functionally illiterate. About 50 percent have had no high-school education. A mere 10 percent are college graduates. This limited amount of formal education not only contributes to technical and intellectual obsolescence so far as work participation is concerned, but also hampers people from using their leisure in interesting, fulfilling ways. For instance, a person who cannot read well (or at all) is not likely to have cultivated broad and stimulating interests that might enrich the retirement years. Do the church's colleges and universities have any responsibility to improve the educational opportunities of these elders of the present, to upgrade their skills and enhance their lives? If they have a responsibility, what can they do?

Some Elders Will Launch Second Careers

As time goes on, more women and men will have the desire and the competence to continue employment or to enter upon second (or third) careers beyond age 65. This will be true of individuals within the faculty and the administration of every college and university. What does this new situation, already on the horizon, say to the personnel policies and practices of the educational institutions of the church? Of course, even as we stress this issue we acknowledge that age per se or even retirement from undergraduate instruction is no bar to continued scholarly endeavor, research, and writing.

The College Has a Role in Training People to Serve Elders

A church college or university has resources to use in assisting in training personnel to work in health and social service agencies and institutions that render direct services to the elderly. Such training might take place either in the regular curriculum or in special teaching sessions and seminars away from the campus. Effective programming can grow out of consultation with church agencies and institutions, with those operated under other private and public auspices, and with gerontology centers and relevant government offices.

Any special approaches to elders (or middle-aged adults) as teachers and learners should recognize that they may have characteristics that differ from those of the young. Elders tend to be self-directing rather than just emerging from dependence. They have accumulated a reservoir of experience that can be a resource for further learning. Their time perspective is changing from one of postponed application of knowledge to one of immediate application. Their orientation to learning moves increasingly from subject-centeredness to an interest in the relationship of a subject to their tasks and social roles.

The growing need for innovative types of education for elders should be an occasion not of frustration but rather of stimulating new challenges in curriculum and campus life in the colleges and universities of the church.

Campus Ministries

Campus ministries sponsored by the Lutheran churches facilitate the work not only of chaplains in Lutheran colleges and universities, but also of full-time and part-time campus pastors in other educational institutions throughout the United States and Canada. Obviously, this large group of key leaders makes up a different audience from the faculty and administrative personnel of LCA-related colleges and universities. It is assumed, nevertheless, that the suggestions made to the latter group are applicable also to the institutions that

campus ministry people serve. They are urged to examine the concepts and suggestions discussed in the previous section and relate
them creatively to the settings in which they work.

Church Camps and Conference Centers

Approximately 160 camps and conference centers in the United
States and Canada are related to the LCA. One-sixth of them report
programs planned for older adults. It is likely that older adults are
included in other general activities.

The Illinois Synod's Lutheran Outdoor Ministries Center conducts
retreats for senior citizens in the spring and the fall. With about
thirty persons usually in attendance, the agenda consists of Bible
study, worship, nature study, hikes, arts and crafts, and good food.
The topics are not slanted toward older persons as such, but
rather have to do with contemporary issues and discussions of Scrip-
ture. Planners discovered long ago that elders tire quickly of dealing
with age-related problems and concerns, that they appreciate instead
the spirited intellectual and physical refreshment of a basic retreat.

Lutheran Outdoor Ministries offers one-day events for groups,
including older adults, throughout the year. In the summer a one-day
fun experience enables older men and women to interact with
younger campers.

The director, Jack Swanson, states that one benefit a camp may
receive from working with elders is the discovery of some special gifts
and gifted people. An older participant revealed that he was a sculp-
tor. "I showed him a seven-foot walnut log we wanted carved. The
end result was a fantastic sculpture of St. Francis of Assisi."[35]

Camps and conference centers like this offer excellent opportunities for elders to study and learn in the midst of good fellowship, and
also to participate actively in informal experiences that bring the
generations together. What a fine setting in which to foster deeper
understanding between young and old.

Resources to Assist
Church Educational Leaders

There are many resources to which educational leaders can turn as
they initiate programs that relate positively to aging and the older
adult.

First, a wealth of published material in gerontology is available, ranging from the popular to the scholarly, from pamphlets to periodicals to audio-visuals to books. These materials may be related to many disciplines, such as psychology, anthropology, sociology, economics, or political science.[36]

Second, conferences, schools, and workshops are held frequently and in all parts of Canada and the United States by national and provincial/state gerontology organizations, university institutes of gerontology, churches, and other groups. Seminary and college faculty members and leaders of campus ministries and outdoor ministries will do well to take advantage of these increasing opportunities.

Third, the academic institutes of gerontology, for example, Duke, Michigan, Oregon, Southern California, Syracuse, and many more (their number and quality are growing), not only provide instructional opportunities, but are likely willing to enter into working relationships with church institutions and also to give counsel in the setting up of viable gerontology programs.[37]

Finally, help may be obtained from LCA churchwide agencies that carry responsibilities in aging. Inquiries should be made to the appropriate agency depending on the nature of the question: Division for Mission in North America, 231 Madison Ave., New York, N.Y. 10016; Division for Parish Services or Division for Professional Leadership, 2900 Queen Lane, Philadelphia, Pa. 19129. Other denominations have comparable boards, commissions, or divisions concerned with aging and the older adult.

Elders and Churchwide Agencies and Regional Judicatories

Most denominations assist and broaden the ministry of their congregations through two basic types of structure:

- regional judicatories — synods, districts, dioceses, presbyteries; and
- churchwide agencies — boards, divisions, commissions, offices.

Educational institutions and social ministry agencies and institutions relate to the various denominations in different ways: to individuals or congregations, to regional judicatories, to churchwide agencies.

These structures beyond congregations all have important roles in enabling the denomination to respond to the challenge of an aging church in an aging society. The knowledge and understanding, sensitivity and creativity of the officers, staff members, and volunteer leaders in churchwide agencies and regional judicatories will have profound influence — positive or negative — on all facets of the church's ministry involving aging and the older adult.

The two types of structure work together closely in responding to the challenges of the demographic revolution, the changes taking place in older adults, and the church's theological understanding. We shall treat them separately, however, as we make suggestions concerning their roles.

Regional Judicatories

The regional judicatory, as an expression of the church, should meet the issues of aging in such ways as the following:

1. Assist congregations to encourage their members to appreciate the whole span of life, to see their own aging as part of God's plan for living, and to rejoice in the multigenerational nature of the community of faith.

2. Counsel congregations seeking pastors to consider men and women of various ages, including some of older years, as candidates. Parishes need to be reminded that persons in their forties, fifties, and sixties normally have a great deal more to give to their ministry than they did when they were younger. Furthermore, the ability to work effectively with youth is not the peculiar possession of clergy and laity who are themselves young, anymore than only older persons can deal with elders. These talents have more to do with personality, sensitivity, and outlook on life than with age.

3. Give fair consideration, when selecting members of the judicatory staff, to women and men who are older. A judicatory relates to people of all ages, including the young-old and the old-old.

4. Encourage the selection of older women and men — since there is no age for retirement from volunteer work — to judicatory committees and to delegations to conventions.

5. Work to develop teamwork among congregations, health and social service agencies and institutions, colleges and seminaries, campus ministries and outdoor ministries that will both serve the needs and draw on the resources of elders within the context of the community of faith.

6. Provide guidance and leadership for general programs and seminars on such topics as the aging process, avoidable factors that accelerate aging, attitudes toward aging, preretirement planning, and viable parish programming.

7. Sponsor training workshops for pastors and other persons involved in ministry with elders, seeking assistance — when feasible — from health and welfare agencies, educational institutions, and/or gerontology centers.

8. Maintain supportive relationships with church-related health and social service agencies and institutions that serve the elderly. As part of cooperative efforts to secure sufficient funds for their work, assist them in encouraging provincial/state and local governments to establish adequate levels of reimbursement for covered services provided to eligible recipients by the agencies and institutions.

9. Cooperate with governmental and nongovernmental organizations engaged in the field of aging by supporting them in their work, engaging in constructive criticism, using their resources, and referring individuals and agencies to them when appropriate, and advo-

cating actions by such organizations that protect the rights, meet the needs, and open up ministry opportunities for older men and women.

10. Establish a supportive fellowship of retired pastors/professional leaders and spouses, widows, and widowers. Several LCA synods have initiated such programs.[38] It is important to include pastors and other leaders from other judicatories who are living in the territory; and to recognize that the most vulnerable group consists of the widowed, who often lose touch with meaningful church relationships beyond their local congregations.

11. Assign responsibility for the ministry with aging and the older adult to a specific program unit, new or existing, and include elders, along with men and women of other ages, in its planning and leadership.

Churchwide Agencies

Denominations vary widely in the names and responsibilities they assign to their churchwide boards, divisions, offices, or commissions. Following is a series of suggestions as to how such agencies, as expressions of the church, can help meet the issues of aging and the older adult. Presented in generic terms, they are listed according to the broad outlines of the LCA Program Structure. It is hoped that creative thinking will give birth to other suggestions.

Grow in Faith and Witness

1. Include issues relating to aging and the older adult as subjects for social analysis and publications from time to time, and as a component, when relevant, of studies and publications on other issues.

2. Make certain that elders and the aging process are referred to in natural and constructive ways in resources prepared for fields such as worship, music, evangelism, education, stewardship, social ministry, laity ministry in daily life and work, leadership development, architecture and art, and ecumenical activities.

3. Incorporate an appreciation of the whole life cycle, including the older years, into
  • the entire curriculum for all ages,
  • specific curriculum material for elders,
  • guidance for visiting, understanding aging, and particular programs, and

- worship materials that meet individual needs, including those of older adults.

4. Help individual Christians (through the printed word, audio-visual aids, etc.) struggle with the searching questions of how to live each stage of life fully and how to face illness and death.[39]

5. Consider including the category of age along with race and sex in guidelines that seek to eliminate stereotypic and demeaning language and imagery from church publications.

6. Include the component of aging and the older adult in work with judicatory staff and parish services committees, and in training events for all phases of parish life — educational ministry, evangelical outreach, stewardship, and congregational social ministry.

7. Include aging also in training events and program development for specialized areas, such as

- new mission congregations,
- town and country congregations,
- urban congregations,
- parish life and ministry development,
- exceptional persons,
- minority group concerns,
- ministry of the laity, and
- media use in congregational outreach.

8. Encourage the development and use of the leadership ability, individual skills, and personal resources of older adults in the total ministry of the church.[40]

9. Lessen feelings of isolation and alienation often experienced by older adults in our society and promote understanding of the need for expression of intimacy among elders.[41]

10. Assist and become advocates for men and women who experience radical changes in life, loss of social and self-esteem, physical and emotional impairment, injustices, and extreme economic disadvantages because of their age.[42]

11. Promote and nurture the general spiritual well-being of older adults through all the ministry functions of the church and other aspects of church life.[43]

12. Strengthen the bonds of family ties and promote intergenerational relationships.[44]

13. Encourage Faith and Life Institutes on aging. They might engage people of various ages discussing lifelong aging in an inter-

generational setting, elders sharing their experiences of the older years and seeking to discover the meaning of vocation for them, or men and women in their forties or fifties looking ahead to retirement.

Reach Out with the Gospel

14. Emphasize the inclusion of elders among the active participants and among the people approached in all evangelical outreach. There are as many older adults as persons of any other age-group among the unchurched and the inactive.

15. Continue the practice of establishing new congregations in communities where older adults are present in sizable numbers.

16. Encourage new congregations to involve elders in leadership from the beginning.

17. Continue to stress free access and mobility for aged and disabled persons in the construction and renovation of buildings used by congregations and church-related institutions.

18. Take into consideration, as regional strategies are developed, the large number of elders likely to be living in the areas involved.

19. Lift up the dimension of aging and the ministry with older adults as integral parts of all overseas work of the church. This should be true of the ministry of proclaiming the gospel, the service of people through social ministry and health care, the recruitment of professional and volunteer personnel, and the efforts to combat injustice.

20. Include relevant news and information about elders in news releases. Feature the concerns of aging and the older adult from time to time in films, videotapes, radio and television programs. It is worth observing that elders probably constitute a large proportion of the listeners to the "Protestant Hour" and similar programs. Such programs afford an opportunity to respond to their needs and also to help all listeners see that aging is a natural process that affects everyone throughout life.

21. Publish in the principal church magazine as often as feasible news and feature articles that foster a positive concept of the total life span, wholesome intergenerational relationships, both the problems and the strengths of older men and women, and the need for elders to be involved, within the limits of interests and strength, in the mainstream of church and society.

22. Continue to include a balanced emphasis upon aging in the books, audio-visuals, and other materials produced. The publishing arm of the church has significant opportunity to convey the constructive ideas and attitudes about aging and the older adult for which the current study is pleading.

23. Consider the tremendous potential that an auxiliary of the church has to influence the thinking of large numbers of people in the church, through its magazine and program materials, its assemblies and conventions, and its workshops training leaders for their tasks. It is hoped that this strength will be employed for the benefit of the older segment of the church and the community without neglecting other important concerns.

Serve Needs in Society

24. Take cognizance of the elder component when joining with other organizations to provide resources for community development through minority economic development, housing coalitions for low- and middle-income families, community organizations, and disaster relief.

25. Assist church-related health and social service agencies and institutions to explore creative ways of ministering with elders, serving them competently as their needs become evident, but also drawing on their resources of talent and time for the fulfillment of the church's mission in the world.[45]

26. Give special attention to the needs and situations of elders in minority groups and those who are poor or in ill health, and make certain that an adequate share of facilities and programs of the church are directed to their benefit.

27. Voice particular concern for the situation of older women. A decisive majority of the population age 65 and over, they often have urgent problems of poverty as well as of loss and loneliness. Very many older women in the church have deep commitment to Christ and should be encouraged to share their talents in the congregation and the community.

28. Recognize clearly the major needs of older persons who are women and members of minority groups, as the church focuses attention upon the need for justice affecting these groups. As the church functions as an advocate in behalf of these and other people, it should

see itself actually as standing in solidarity with them as they press their own case in the halls of government. Furthermore, the church and elders themselves should view this kind of advocacy, in which they promote their own cause, as part of the larger struggle for justice for *all people.*

29. Be alert to the genuine problems of older adults when dealing with such societal issues as criminal justice, health care, equal employment opportunity, investment decisions, tax policy, poverty and hunger, and world community.

30. Assist congregations, coalitions of congregations, and community organizations to engage actively in social ministry projects that are meaningful to older adults as both participants and beneficiaries.[46]

31. Encourage congregations and coalitions to sponsor senior citizen centers as vital sources of activity for individual and community betterment.

32. Urge congregations or groups of congregations to arrange preretirement courses, seminars, etc. An excellent guide is *Ten to Get Ready*, by Betty Wolf and Umhau Wolf, Fortress Press, 2900 Queen Lane, Philadelphia, Pa. 19129 (1977).

33. Work with church-related colleges and campus ministries to include a balanced treatment of older adults and the aging process in regular and special courses, continuing education, and field work, and to engage elders as faculty, students, and invited resource persons.[47]

Cooperate with Other Communities of Faith

34. Realize the importance of working with other groups. In the church's ministry with aging and the older adult, strength and stimulation are gained from working with other churches and religious organizations directly or through such instruments as the National Interfaith Coalition on Aging, the National (U.S.) and Canadian Councils of Churches, and the world organizations in the field. The issues of aging are relevant at many points as churches reach out to each other in ecumenical relationships.

35. Cooperate with other groups (not strictly appropriate under the heading of "Communities of Faith") in activities that promote justice, relieve misery, and reconcile the estranged. This includes national governmental and nongovernmental groups in the United

States and Canada and many regional and local organizations that have significance in the area of gerontology.

Develop Professional Leadership

36. Encourage theological seminaries to include education in the field of aging as a part of the training of pastors and other professional leaders of the church.[48]

37. Include elders when recruiting lay professionals for church positions.

38. Make the fullest possible use of the Growth in Ministry program (LCA Division for Professional Leadership) for the assistance of pastors and other professional leaders. The Preretirement Workshop within this program is appropriately offered for the benefit of those who look ahead to retirement, including not only parish pastors and leaders but overseas missionaries, institutional and military chaplains, and judicatory and churchwide agency personnel. The Model A Workshop, "Refocusing: A Look at Life and Ministry," is intended for career assessment at different ages. Since it will reach pastors and other professional leaders at earlier ages than the Preretirement Workshops (some younger leaders are not likely to participate in the latter) it should help many persons make lifetime plans, including those for aging and retirement, in the context of career planning.

39. Continue publishing in the professional leadership magazines (*Partners* in the LCA) enlightening articles that convey a constructive view of aging.

40. Support theological seminaries, colleges, and synods in including offerings in continuing education that will aid pastors and other professional leaders in understanding aging, recognizing the strengths and the needs of older people, and initiating effective parish ministry that includes this dimension of life.

41. Seek ways to provide financial assistance for training persons for careers in gerontology within the church.

42. Continue gathering and evaluating retirement statistics concerning pastors and other professional leaders. Distribute helpful material like the LCA's "Guidelines for Retired Clergy."

43. Encourage all regional judicatories to organize supportive fellowships of retired pastors/professional leaders and spouses, widows and widowers. A churchwide agency might evaluate the fellowships

that already exist, and suggest several patterns that judicatories could adapt to their own situations.

44. Manifest active concern for both the needs and the potential of the elders who live and work within the Deaconess Community.

45. Include institutional and military chaplains in programs that provide education and sensitizing to the issues of aging and the older adult, since they have frequent opportunity both to minister to elders and to influence the insights of younger people into aging as a life-long experience. Chaplains themselves will benefit from preretirement education and counseling.

46. Continue providing preretirement education and counseling to overseas missionaries. When missionaries retire many of them have not only the normal problems of adjusting to retirement but the additional problems of reentry into North American culture after years in other lands.

47. Engage in a careful review of current pension and health benefit policies and practices in terms of the descriptive materials in Part One, "Elders Today and Tomorrow."

Support of the Organization

48. Enforce personnel policies firmly, so that churchwide agencies refrain from all employment discrimination on account of age.

49. Publicize projects involving older adults as possible recipients of special funding gifts, through such activities as the LCA Foundation, Designated Advance Giving, and the LCA World Hunger Appeal.

50. Give the same consideration to the older segment of the population as to other segments in regional judicatory, churchwide agency, and churchwide planning.

Organizing for Leadership

The magnitude of the challenge articulated in this study calls for a response that is strong and creative, both in the churchwide agencies and in the regional judicatories. Two primary principles should guide those who will determine the structure of leadership:

    a. Recognition that all facets of this church and its synods are involved in dealing with the concerns of aging and the older adult. For many years the church's approach was to see "aging" as a problem and to initiate programs under the social ministry rubric. Hence, a large number of nursing homes, retirement centers, and service agencies under church auspices appeared. Even advocacy on behalf of older people was an extension of the service function. In recent decades the church has come to realize that service to elders, though very important, is not enough and is frequently inappropriate. There must be a new emphasis upon aging as a lifelong process and upon elders today and tomorrow as a group that is rapidly increasing in numbers and changing in characteristics.

This study has explored the implications of the demographic revolution, along with Christian theological imperatives, not only for social ministry but for all expressions of this church's life and ministry. It has emphasized that within the church the responsibility for facing the challenge of aging and the older adult is lodged in nearly every program area. Thus, the instrument known as a staff team is proper, since it periodically brings together staff representatives from several churchwide agencies. A Staff Team on Aging facilitates the sharing of information, the coordination of programs, and the stimulation of new programs in churchwide agencies.

The same kind of device is appropriate in each judicatory. There, too, aging is a topic that crosses into all areas of responsibility; it should be consciously addressed in various committees, commissions, and task forces.

b. The clear designation of at least one person to work full time in this field. This person should have special education and experience in gerontology and the capacity to give vigorous leadership. He or she should chair the Staff Team on Aging, and have the ability to work effectively with other persons in churchwide agencies, judicatories, and other parts of the church. If the church is to give priority to its response to the issues of an aging church in an aging society, it is essential that a qualified leader be specifically assigned the task and be given the time and the support to do it with the energy it deserves. This key leader would be assisted greatly by an advisory committee appointed from the constituency. Members should be men and women from different age groups, different racial, ethnic, economic, and social backgrounds, and exhibiting different qualifications.

It is to be hoped that each judicatory will likewise give a definite assignment of responsibility to one person, or at least to a strong committee or task force.

A Final Word

The concerns of aging and the older adult are not peripheral but essential parts of the business of the church. Whether we speak of the lifelong aging of all people or the specific experiences of those who are in the older years, we speak of deeply human concerns that have a great deal to do with living. In these the church is inevitably involved.

Frederick J. Schumacher writes: "The fundamental human question of the meaning of life, of happiness, of the need to feel fulfillment are the central problems of aging. These issues are precisely the subject matter of theology. If the Christian gospel does not have the life-giving word for the aging, then there is no life-giving word. While the church cannot neglect speaking to such issues as adequate income and housing, if all of these were satisfied, the . . . theological dimensions would still remain."[1]

Although the church has always responded to the needs and challenges of older men and women there is today an urgency for the church to respond in new ways to elders. Their numbers are growing dramatically, both in the general population and in the membership of the church. Also, the characteristics of older adults are changing, perhaps just as dramatically. As we move toward and into the next century, elders will be better educated, will have better health, and will be more assertive in assuming leadership and taking active part in life around them.

We should listen to these elders and let them teach us. We should let them teach us about a way of life that is freed from the societal requirement to be productive and to conform. We should let them teach us about an understanding of life limited by losses and defined by death but lifted up in victory by the resurrection of Christ. Many elders cannot be teachers like this. But in our midst there are those whose reflections upon the human experience in the light of God's Word make them teachers to whom we must listen.

The church's response to aging and the older adult has to be positive, constructive, creative. This includes compassionate action to meet the needs of the frail and vulnerable. It includes standing alongside elders in aggressive advocacy for justice in public policy, the media, and cultural attitudes. Above all, to be positive in its response the church has to see older adults, regardless of their conditions, as persons of dignity and individuality, persons who have not only problems but potential, persons who in most cases are able to make distinctive contributions to both church and society.

The response should come from every part of the church—individuals and congregations; educational, health, and social service agencies and institutions; regional judicatories and churchwide agencies. And the church should engage elders in every facet of its ministry—worship and evangelism, education and social ministry, stewardship and finance—wherever talent, strength, and willingness may lead.

The priesthood of the baptized is no respecter of age. Older women and men who are baptized are in every sense members of the holy Christian people, the community of faith.

Notes

INTRODUCTION

1. Frederick R. Eisele, Preface to special issue on "Political Consequences of Aging," *The Annals of American Academy of Political and Social Science* (September 1974), ix.

2. Landon Jones, "The Baby-Boom Legacy," *Saturday Evening Post* (May/June 1982): 20ff.

3. Simone de Beauvoir, in her classic, *The Coming of Age*, says: "Old age can only be understood as a whole; it is not solely a biological, but also a cultural fact," trans. Patrick O'Brian (New York: G. P. Putnam's Sons, 1972), 13.

4. David Hackett Fischer, *Growing Old in America* (New York and Oxford: Oxford University Press, 1978). This summary is based primarily on Fischer's book, which speaks only about the United States and only about national history since the year 1607. It is likely that the principal themes were similar in Canada. Another fine book on the history of aging is W. Andrew Achenbaum, *Old Age in the New Land* (Baltimore and London: Johns Hopkins University Press, 1978).

PART ONE
ELDERS TODAY AND TOMORROW

1. *Chartbook on Aging in America*, produced by the U.S. Dept. of Health and Human Services for the 1981 White House Conference on Aging. Most U.S. statistics in this study come from the *Chartbook*.

2. *Fact Book on Aging in Canada* (1983) prepared by the Canadian Dept. of National Health and Welfare for the Second Canadian Conference on Aging. Most Canadian statistics in this study come from the *Fact Book*.

3. The United Church of Christ, as a result of a congregational survey, reports that persons 65 and older constitute 23 percent of its membership. The figure is probably similar in the LCA and other major denominations.

4. Bernice L. Neugarten, "Age Groups in American Society and the Rise of the Young-Old," *The Annals of American Academy of Political and Social Science* (September 1974), 187–98. Some gerontologists speak of "young-old" as 60–75, "middle-old," 75–85, and "old-old," 85 and beyond. Despite the variations, Professor Neugarten's description is sufficient for this study.

5. *Lutheran Book of Worship* (Minneapolis: Augsburg Publishing House; Philadelphia: Board of Publication, Lutheran Church in America, 1978), 44.

6. Ethel Shanas, "Family Help Patterns and Social Class in Three Countries," in *Middle Age and Aging*, ed. Bernice L. Neugarten (Chicago and London: University of Chicago Press, 1968), 196–305.

7. Peter Townsend, "The Emergence of the Four-Generation Family," in ibid., 255–57. Townsend estimates that more than 40 percent of U.S. families 65 and over have great-grandchildren.

8. A fuller development of the three sources of meaning is found in Leslie A. Morgan, "Aging in a Family Context," in *Aging: Prospects and Issues*, ed. Richard H. Davis, 3d ed. (Los Angeles: University of Southern California Press, 1981), 98–100.

9. The statistics quoted do not include a very large number of instances of self-neglect, reported by 82 percent of the respondents to the survey.

10. Gray Panther *Network* (July/August 1983), 15.

11. *Elder Abuse*, prepared by U.S. Department of Health and Human Services (May 1980) (DHHS Publication No. 81–20152, Government Printing Office, Washington, D.C.).

12. Roy H. Rodgers, *Family Interaction and Transaction: The Developmental Approach* (Englewood Cliffs, N.J.: Prentice-Hall, 1972). Referred to in Allen J. Moore, "The Family Relations of Older Persons," in *Ministry with the Aging*, ed. William J. Clements (New York: Harper & Row, 1981).

13. Moore, "Family Relations of Older Persons."

14. James D. Manney, Jr., *Aging in American Society* (Ann Arbor: The Institute of Gerontology, The University of Michigan–Wayne State University, 1975), 125.

15. Ibid., 126.

16. Some private pension funds permit a person to select benefit options without consulting the spouse, thus making it possible for the spouse to be cut out of survival benefits. Furthermore, the provisions of pension plans are often described poorly or not at all to prospective beneficiaries. Perhaps there should be serious study of such proposals as earning-sharing under U.S. Social Security, whereby a husband's earnings would be divided 50–50 for the calculation of benefits.

17. Whereas the total U.S. population 65 and over has increased about eightfold since 1900, the population 85 and over has grown to 22 times its size at the turn of the century. *Chartbook on Aging in America*, 6. The same trend is found in Canada. *Fact Book on Aging in Canada*, 18.

18. Correspondence with Clifton L. Monk, retired consultant to the LCA–Canada Section and the LCA Division for Mission in North America.

19. William J. Hanna, "Advocacy and the Elderly," in *Aging*, ed. Davis, 315.

20. Cynthia M. Taeuber, "The Past, Present, and Future: A Review of Demographic Trends in the United States," unpublished address to the Religion Research Association and the Society for Scientific Study of Religion, 30 October 1981.

21. Neal E. Cutler, "The Aging Population and Social Policy," in *Aging*, ed. Davis, 249.

22. Ibid., 254.

23. Ibid.

24. Age 65 was selected in 1935 when the Social Security Act was drafted. It may be based on German Chancellor Otto von Bismarck's 1870 decision that 65 was the proper age for retirement of public servants.

25. Cutler, "Aging Population," 254–55.

26. Robert N. Butler discusses the myths much more fully on pages 32–34 of his book, *Why Survive? Being Old in America* (New York: Harper & Row, 1975).

27. There have been recent reports in the media of advances in the diagnosis and treatment of Alzheimer's disease, one of the most serious and prevalent of brain syndromes.

28. Arthritis (44 percent of persons 65 and older), hypertension (39 percent), hearing impairments (28 percent), heart conditions (27 percent) visual impairments (12 percent), and diabetes (8 percent). *Chartbook on Aging in America*, 80, quoting from 1979 National Center for Health Statistics survey.

29. Ages 65–74, 4.8 visits per year; 75 and over, 5.1 visits; under 65, 3.2 visits. The pattern of dental visits is in sharp contrast: 44 percent of elders have not seen a dentist in five or more years. This situation probably exists because of the minimal availability of reimbursement. Ibid., 82. It has been suggested that elders often visit the doctor's office because the presence of people in the waiting room helps relieve their loneliness.

30. Manney, *Aging in American Society*, 148.

31. Ibid., 147.

32. Karl A. Schneider, *Alcoholism and Addiction* (Philadelphia: Fortress Press, 1976), 10.

33. Manney, *Aging in American Society*, 146.

34. Alan Cranston, "Progress in Controlling the Aging Process," *USA Today* (May 1980), 18.

35. Ibid., 17–18.

36. It is not yet clear how nursing homes will change as a result of the new system of third-party reimbursement of hospitals for patient care at a flat fee for each of 467 categories of illness, usually regardless of how long they stay in the hospital. The system is called Diagnostic Related Groups (DRG). It is likely that nursing homes will have to be prepared to care for people who have been discharged from the hospital earlier than was formerly the case. Hospitals today are establishing or buying nursing homes themselves.

37. Proposals have been made for reverse annuity mortgages, which would make it possible for homeowners to obtain monthly incomes through loans on their mortgages.

38. More older persons in the United States now live in the suburbs than in the central cities (33 vs. 30 percent). Proportionately, however, 55 percent of metropolitan-dwelling older whites are in the suburbs, while 75 percent of metropolitan older blacks live in the central cities. Numerically, there are almost 6 million older whites to 1 million older blacks in central cities. *Chartbook on Aging in America*, 116.

39. Donald O. Cowgill, "Aging in Population and Societies," *The Annals of American Academy of Political and Social Science* (September 1974), 13.

40. Jones, "Baby-Boom Legacy."

41. Kathy Serock, Carol Seefeldt, Richard K. Jantz, and Alice Galper, "As Children See Old Folks," *The Journal* of the National Education Association (March-April 1977). These authors report that comprehensive surveys reveal that most children have very limited contact with older people outside their families. They express such stereotypes as: "The old are all wrinkled and short," "They have gray hair," "They don't go out much," "They chew funny," "Old people sit all day and watch TV in their rocking chairs," and "They have heart attacks and die."

42. Taeuber, "Past, Present, and Future."

43. M. H. Beach, "Business and the Graying of America," *Vital Speeches* (June 1, 1981), 488–92.

44. For an excellent description of the fundamental changes needed to accomplish this intermingling see Butler, *Why Survive?* 384ff.

45. *Canada Handbook* (1979), 42.

46. Robert H. Binstock, "Aging and the Future of American Politics," *The Annals of American Academy of Political and Social Science* (September 1974), 203.

47. The images of older adults portrayed on prime-time television dramatize the pervasive stereotypes. Conspicuous examples are Johnny Carson's "Aunt Blabby" and Carol Burnett's old couple sitting side by side in their rockers. According to a ten-year study by the University of Pennsylvania's Annenberg School of Communications, only one out of every fifty fictional TV characters is over 65, and a decisive majority of those who do appear are presented in negative ways. They come across as stubborn, eccentric, ineffectual, sexuality inactive, and often downright silly. Evidently the producers do not take seriously the fact that, according to A. C. Nielsen, men and women over 55 watch more TV than any other group.

48. Neugarten, "Age Groups in American Society," 197–98.

49. Douglas W. Nelson, "The Meanings of Old Age for Public Policy," *National Forum*, the Phi Kappa Phi Journal (fall 1982), 27ff. Subsequent references to Nelson are from this article.

PART TWO
THE CHURCH'S RESPONSE

1. Social Statement adopted by the Lutheran Church in America, Ninth Biennial Convention, Chicago, Illinois, 12–19 July 1978.

2. Carl G. Howie, "Theology for Aging." in *Spiritual Well-Being of the Elderly*, ed. James A. Thorson and Thomas C. Cook, Jr. (Springfield, Ill.: Charles C. Thomas, 1980), 66. Several ideas in these paragraphs were stimulated by Howie's chapter as well as by the LCA Social Statement, "Aging and the Older Adult."

3. Howie, "Theology for Aging," 68.

4. Robert M. Gray and David O. Moberg, *The Church and the Older Person*, rev. ed. (Grand Rapids: Wm. B. Eerdmans, 1977). 58ff.

5. Maggie Kuhn, in unpublished address to LCA Convocation on Aging, 19–22 October 1973.

6. Robert N. Butler and Myrna I. Lewis, *Aging and Mental Health: Positive Psychosocial Approaches* (St. Louis: C. V. Mosby, 1973). Quoted in Robert N. Butler, *Why Survive? Being Old in America* (New York: Harper & Row, 1975), 12.

7. For more detailed descriptions of these projects consult Donald F. Clingan, *Aging Persons in the Community of Faith* (St. Louis: Christian Board of Publication, 1980); John A. Jorgenson: *Ministry with Older Persons*, a multimedia packet produced by the LCA Division for Parish Services (Philadelphia: Fortress Press, 1975); Robert W. McClellan, *Claiming a Frontier: Ministry and Older People* (Los Angeles: University of Southern California Press, 1977); John A. McConomy, "Ministry with the Aging," in *Word and World: Theology for Christian Ministry* (St. Paul: Luther Northwestern Theological Seminary, Vol II, no. 4 [fall 1982], 386–89; and Cedric W. Tilberg, ed. *The Fullness of Life* (New York: LCA Division for Mission in North America, 1980). Further information may be obtained from the National Council on the Aging, 600 Maryland Ave., S.W., Washington, D.C. 20004.

8. Conversation with Dr. Arthur S. Flemming, former U.S. Commissioner on Aging, on 15 July 1983.

9. Unpublished information secured from Dr. Marcus L. Burr, Jr., pastor of the First Presbyterian Church of Deming, N. Mex. The project reported was conducted in partial fulfillment of requirements for the Doctor of Ministry degree from McCormick Theological Seminary, Chicago, awarded to Pastor Burr on 6 June 1978. Only selected portions of the report are included here.

10. Urban T. Holmes, "Worship and Aging: Memory and Repentance," in *Ministry with the Aging: Designs, Challenges, Foundations*, ed. William M. Clements (New York: Harper & Row, 1981), 91–106.

11. Here the word "liturgy" is used in its profoundest sense. It is derived from the Greek *leitourgia* (ult. from *laos*, "people," + *ergon*, "work"): "work of the people." Public worship is inseparably related to the daily life of the people. As St. Benedict said: *Laborare est orare*, "to work is to pray."

12. For information about "The Caring Community: You Can be a Part of It," write Harold J. Hinrichs, Division for Life and Mission in the Congregation, The American Lutheran Church, 422 S. Fifth St., Minneapolis, Minn. 55415.

13. Write the American Association of Retired Persons, 1909 K Street, N.W., Washington, D.C. 20049.

14. For further reading cf. Robert N. Butler and Myrna I. Lewis *Love and Sex After Sixty* (New York: Harper & Row, 1976) (paperback). Also cf.

Robert L. Solnick, ed., *Sexuality and Aging* (Los Angeles: University of Southern California Press, 1978).

15. American Association of Retired Persons.

16. Cf. LCA Social Statement, "Aging and the Older Adult," section on "Public Policy," Item 1.

17. Betty Wolf and Umhau Wolf, *Ten to Get Ready* (Philadelphia: Parish Life Press [LCA], 1977).

18. LCA Division for Parish Services, 2900 Queen Lane, Philadelphia, Pa. 19129.

19. Fortress Church Supply Stores advertise several excellent intergenerational resources for use in congregations or families. For information contact Fortress at 2900 Queen Lane, Philadelphia, Pa. 19129 (1-800-FORTRES) or the Fortress Store nearest you.

20. National Interfaith Coalition on Aging, 298 South Hull Street (Box 1924), Athens, Ga. 30603.

21. *The Book of Concord*, trans. and ed. by Theodore G. Tappert (Philadelphia: Fortress Press, 1959), 32.

22. *The Church in Social Welfare*, prepared in 1964 by the Commission on the Role of the Church in Social Welfare of the LCA Board of Social Ministry, provides an excellent description of this church's involvement in the field and an examination of relevant issues and questions. LCA Division for Mission in North America, Interpretation Office, 231 Madison Ave., New York, N.Y. 10016.

23. The Social Statement, "The Church and Social Welfare," may be obtained from the DMNA Interpretation Office, 231 Madison Ave., New York, N.Y. 10016.

24. Gray Panther *Network* (July/August 1983), 4.

25. The Board of Social Ministry of the LCA's Minnesota Synod is one agency that is organizing outreach programs in many communities, designed to help elders to continue living in their own homes. *The Lutheran* (March 7, 1984), 20.

26. Lutheran Social Service of Minnesota, for example, reports having made more then 140 such "matches" since 1980. Ibid.

27. See above, "Elders of Tomorrow Will Be Different," 38–47.

28. David Moberg, "Aging and Theological Education," *Theological Education* (winter 1980), 285–86. The specific reference is to David S. Schuller et al., *Readiness for Ministry: Vol. 1 — Criteria* (Vandalia, Ohio: Association of Theological Schools in the U.S. and Canada, 1975).

29. At least five Lutherans participated in Project GIST: Arthur H. Becker and Leland E. Elhard, Trinity Seminary; J. Russell Hale, Gettysburg; Melvin A. Kimble, Luther Northwestern; and Vernon L. Strempke, Pacific. Each of these professors has introduced the subject of aging into his seminary program.

30. *Theological Education*, Vol. 16, Special Issue 3 (winter 1980), is devoted entirely to Project GIST. The Guidelines for Competency Objectives are described on pp. 297–309.

31. Jesse H. Ziegler, "Strategies for Using the Guidelines in Seminary Curricula, in ibid., 351.

32. *Between Classes*, ELDERHOSTEL newsletter, Vol. 1, no. 1 (1983), 3. For full information about course offerings and hostelships (scholarships) write to ELDERHOSTEL, 100 Boylston Street, Boston, Mass. 02116.

33. Harold L. Hodgkinson. "Guess Who's Coming to College," *Academe* (March-April 1983), 19.

34. Richard W. Solberg and Martin P. Strommen, *How Church-Related Are Church-Related Colleges?* (New York: Division for Mission in North America, Lutheran Church in America, 1980), 22–23.

35. Correspondence with the Rev. John E. Swanson, Lutheran Outdoor Ministries Center (Illinois Synod, LCA), P. O. Box 239, Oregon. Ill. 61061.

36. Write the National Council on the Aging for up-to-date information, 600 Maryland Ave., S.W., West Wing 100, Washington, D.C. 20024.

37. For information about gerontology institutes, write the National Council on the Aging; Miss Lola Wilson, Consultant on Aging, Policy Research and Long-Range Planning Branch (Welfare), Ottawa, Ont., Can. K1A 0K9; or the U.S. Department of Health and Human Services, Administration on Aging, 330 C St. S.W., Washington, D.C. 20201.

38. For example, Florida, New Jersey, and Pacific Southwest synods.

39. Goals and Objectives of LCA Division for Parish Services for its ministry with aging, 2900 Queen Lane, Philadelphia, Pa. 19129, #a.

40. Ibid., #f.

41. Ibid., #e.

42. Ibid., #c.

43. Ibid., #g.

44. Ibid., #d.

45. For full discussion see above, "Elders and the Church's Agencies and Institutions," 73–84.

46. For full discussion see above, "Elders in Congregational Life," 55–72.

47. For full discussion see above, "Elders and the Church's Programs of Education — Colleges and Universities," 90–96.

48. For full discussion see above, "Elders and the Church's Programs of Education —Theological Schools," 85–90.

A FINAL WORD

1. Frederick J. Schumacher, pastor of St. Matthew's Lutheran Church, White Plains, N.Y., unpublished thesis submitted in partial fulfillment of the requirements for the degree of Doctor of Ministry, Princeton Theological Seminary, Princeton, N.J. (1978), 2.

DATE DUE

DEC 11 '88			

DEMCO 38-297